OLD M

HOROSCOPE AND ASTRAL DIARY

PISCES

foulsham
LONDON • NEW YORK • TORONTO • SYDNEY

C000072114

foulsham

Capital Point, 33 Bath Road, Slough, Berkshire, SL1 3UF, England

Foulsham books can be found in all good bookshops and direct from
www.foulsham.com

ISBN: 978-0-572-04013-0

A CIP record for this book is available from the British Library

Printed in Great Britain by CPI Group (UK) Ltd, Croydon, CR0 4YY.

CONTENTS

INTRODUCTION

In the midst of our busy lives we often fail to notice the subtle changes within our natures that take place on an almost moment-by-moment basis. Some of these are the natural result of circumstances, but others are a direct response to the constantly changing patterns of the Sun, Moon and planets. Astrology gives us an opportunity to make the very best of what cosmological forces are acting upon us at any particular point in time, and Old Moore has been tracking planetary movements and the bearing they have on humanity for many centuries. The most recent result of his efforts is the Astral Diary for 2013 – a complete book geared specifically towards you and the influences that help to make you what you are.

If you want to know whether a new relationship is likely to turn out the way you hope, whether you are in for a good time in the financial stakes, or whether family pressures could be a problem, Old Moore is the person to ask. The Astral Diary gives you an easy-to-follow daily summary of the way the stars and planets are affecting you, and also tells you what you should be doing now in order to maximise your potential for the future. And there is also space in the diaries for your own comments and appointments.

The Astral Diary allows you to look much deeper into your own individual nature than other yearly forecasts do. Your uniqueness is reflected by the time of day you were born and by the position of specific heavenly bodies such as the Moon and the planet Venus. Using the Astral Diary's unique tables you can work out what makes you tick in a much more personal sense, and can then deal much more effectively with the twists and turns of life.

Every nuance of your nature is captured within your astrological profile, and using the Astral Diary you can get so close to the core of planetary influence that you can almost feel the subtle undertones that, in the end, have a profound bearing on your life and circumstances. It is even possible to register when little Mercury is 'retrograde', which means that it appears to be moving backwards in space when viewed from the Earth. Mercury rules communication, so be prepared to deal with a few setbacks in this area when you see the sign ☿. Used correctly, astrology allows you to maximise your potential, to strike whilst the iron is hot and to live a more contented and successful life. Consulting *Old Moore's Astral Diary* will make you more aware of what really makes you the person you are and is a fascinating way to register the very heartbeat of the solar system of which we are all a part.

Old Moore extends his customary greeting to all people of the Earth and offers his age-old wishes for a happy and prosperous period ahead.

THE ESSENCE OF PISCES

Exploring the Personality of Pisces the Fishes

(20th FEBRUARY – 20th MARCH)

What's in a sign?

Pisceans are fascinating people – everyone you come across is likely to admit that fact. By nature you are kind, loving, trustful and inclined to work very hard on behalf of the people you love – and perhaps even those you don't like very much. Your nature is sympathetic and you will do anything you can to improve the lot of those you consider to be worse off than yourself. There is a very forgiving side to your temperament and also a strong artistic flair that can find an outlet in any one of a dozen different ways.

It's true you are difficult to know, and there is a very important reason for this. Your nature goes deep, so deep in fact that someone would have to live with you for a lifetime to plumb even a part of its fathomless depths. What the world sees is only ever a small part of the total magic of this most compulsive and fascinating zodiac sign. Much of your latent power and natural magic is constantly kept bottled up, because it is never your desire to manipulate those around you. Rather, you tend to wait in the shadows until opportunities to come into your own present themselves. In love you are ardent and sincere, though sometimes inclined to choose a partner too readily and too early. There's a dreamy quality to your nature that makes you easy to adore, but which can also cause difficulties if the practical necessities of life take a very definite second place.

The chances are that you love music and picturesque scenery, and you may also exhibit a definite fondness for animals. You prefer to live in the country rather than in the middle of a noisy and smelly town, and tend to keep a reasonably well-ordered household. Your family can easily become your life and you always need a focus for your energies. You are not at all good at feathering your own nest, unless you know that someone else is also going to benefit on the way. A little more selfishness probably would not go amiss on occasions because you are often far too willing to put yourself out wholesale for people who don't respect your sacrifices. Pisceans can be full of raging passions and are some of the most misunderstood people to be found anywhere within the great circle of the zodiac.

Pisces resources

It is the very essence of your zodiac sign that you are probably sitting there and saying to yourself 'Resources? I have no resources'. Of course you are wrong, though it has to be admitted that a glaring self-confidence isn't likely to be listed amongst them. You are, however, a very deep thinker, and this can turn out to be a great advantage and a useful tool when it comes to getting on in life. Because your natural intuition is so strong (some people would call you psychic), you are rarely fooled by the glib words of others. Your own natural tendency to tell the truth can be a distinct advantage and a great help to you when it comes to getting on in life from a practical and financial viewpoint.

Whilst many of the signs of the zodiac tend to respond to life in an impulsive way, you are more likely to weigh up the pros and cons of any given situation very carefully. This means that when you do take action you can achieve much more success – as well as saving a good deal of energy on the way. People tend to confide in you automatically, so you are definitely at an advantage when it comes to knowing what makes your family and friends tick. At work you can labour quietly and confidently, either on your own or in the company of others. Some people would assert that Pisceans are model employees because you really do not know how to give anything less than your best.

Never underestimate the power of your instincts. Under most circumstances you are aware of the possible outcome of any given situation and should react as your inner mind dictates. Following this course inevitably puts you ahead of the game and explains why so quiet a sign can promote so many winners in life. Not that you are particularly competitive. It's much more important for you to be part of a winning team than to be out there collecting the glory for yourself.

You are dependable, kind, loving and peerless in your defence of those you take to. All of these are incredible resources when used in the correct way. Perhaps most important of all is your ability to get others on your side. In this you cannot be matched.

Beneath the surface

Everyone instinctively knows that there is something very important going on beneath the surface of the Piscean mind, though working out exactly what it might be is a different kettle of fish altogether. The fact is that you are very secretive about yourself and tend to give very little away. There are occasions when this tendency can be a saving grace, but others where it is definitely a great disadvantage. What isn't hard to see is your natural sympathy and your desire to help those in trouble. There's no end gain here, it's simply the way you are. Your inspiration to do anything is rarely rooted in what your own prize is likely to be. In your soul you are poetical, deeply romantic and inextricably tied to the forces and cycles of the world that brought you to birth.

Despite your capacity for single-minded concentration in some matters, you are often subject to mental confusion. Rational considerations often take second place to intuitive foresight and even inspiration. Making leaps in logic isn't at all unusual for you and forms part of the way you judge the world and deal with it.

If you really want to get on in life, and to gain the most you can from your interactions with others, you need to be very truthful in your approach. Somehow or other that means finding out what is really going on in your mind and explaining it to those around you. This is never going to be an easy process, partly because of your naturally secretive ways. Actually some astrologers overplay the tendency of Pisces to keep its secrets. A great deal of the time you simply don't think you have anything to say that would interest others and you always lack confidence in your own judgements. This is a shame because you rarely proceed without thinking carefully and don't often make glaring mistakes.

Many Pisceans develop an ingrained tendency to believe themselves inadequate in some way. Once again this is something you should fight against. Knowing others better, and allowing them to get to know you, might cause you to feel less quirky or strange. Whether you realise it or not you have a natural magnetism that draws others towards you. Try to spend rather less time thinking – though without losing that Piscean ability to meditate which is central to your well-being. If you allow the fascinating world of the Piscean mind to be shared by the people you come to trust, you should become more understandable to people who really want to like you even more.

Making the best of yourself

It must be remembered that the zodiac sign of Pisces represents two Fishes, tethered by a cord but constantly trying to break away from each other. This says a great deal about the basic Piscean nature. The inward, contemplative side of your personality is often at odds with the more gregarious and chatty qualities you also possess. Learning about this duality of nature can go at least part of the way towards dealing with it.

Although you often exhibit a distinct lack of self-confidence in your dealings with the world at large, you are, at heart, quite adept, flexible and able to cope under almost any circumstance. All that is really required in order to have a positive influence on life and to be successful is for you to realise what you are capable of achieving. Alas this isn't quite as easy as it might appear, because the introspective depths of your nature make you think too much and cause you to avoid the very actions that would get you noticed more. This can be something of a dilemma for Pisces, though it is certainly not insurmountable.

Never be afraid to allow your sensitivity to show. It is one of your greatest assets and it is part of the reason why other people love you so much – far more, in fact, than you probably realise. Your natural warmth, grace and charm are certain to turn heads on those occasions when you can't avoid being watched. The creative qualities that you possess make it possible for you to manufacture harmonious surroundings, both for yourself and for your family, who are very important to you. At the same time you recognise the practical in life and don't mind getting your hands dirty, especially when it comes to helping someone else out of a mess.

One of the best ruses Pisceans can use in order to get over the innate shyness that often attends the sign is to put on an act. Pisceans are very good natural actors and can easily assume the role of another individual. So, in your dealings with the world at large, manufacture a more confident individual, though without leaving out all the wonderful things that make you what you are now. Play this part for all you are worth and you will then truly be making the best of yourself.

The impressions you give

There is absolutely no doubt that you are more popular, admired and even fancied than you could ever believe. Such is the natural modesty of your zodiac sign that you invariably fail to pick up on those little messages coming across from other people that say 'I think you are wonderful'. If we don't believe in ourselves it's difficult for us to accept that others think we are worth their consideration. Failing to realise your worth to the world at large is likely to be your greatest fault and needs to be corrected. In a way it doesn't matter, when seen from the perspective of others. What they observe is a warm-hearted individual. Your magnetic personality is always on display, whether you intend it to be or not, which is another reason why you tend to attract far more attention than you would sometimes elicit. Most Pisceans are quite sexy, another quality that is bound to come across to the people you meet, at least some of whom would be willing to jump through hoops if you were to command it.

In short, what you show, and what you think you are, could be two entirely different things. If you don't believe this to be the case you need to carry out a straw poll amongst some of the people you know. Ask them to write down all your qualities as they see them. The result will almost certainly surprise you and demonstrate that you are far more capable, and loveable, than you believe yourself to be. Armed with this knowledge you can walk forward in life with more confidence and feel as content inside as you appear to be when viewed by the world at large.

People rely heavily on you. That much at least you will have noticed in a day-to-day sense. They do so because they know how well you deal with almost any situation. Even in a crisis you show your true colours and that's part of the reason why so many Piscean people find themselves involved in the medical profession. You are viewed as being stronger than you believe yourself to be, which is why everyone tends to be so surprised when they discover that you are vulnerable and inclined to worry.

The way forward

You have a great deal to offer the world, even if you don't always appreciate how much. Although you are capable of being shy and introverted on occasions, you are equally likely to be friendly, chatty and very co-operative. You settle to just about any task, though you do possess a sense of freedom that makes it difficult for you to be cooped up in the same place for days and weeks at a stretch. You prefer the sort of tasks that allow your own natural proclivities to shine out, and you exhibit an instinctive creative tendency in almost anything you do.

Use your natural popularity to the full. People are always willing to put themselves out on your behalf, mainly because they know how generous you are and want to repay you for some previous favour. You should never be too proud to accept this sort of proffered help and must avoid running away with the idea that you are unequal to any reasonable task that you set yourself.

It's true that some of your thoughts are extremely deep and that you can get yourself into something of a brown study on occasions, which can be translated by the world around you as depression. However, you are far more stable than you probably believe yourself to be because Pisces is actually one of the toughest of the zodiac signs.

Because you are born of a Water sign it is likely that you would take great delight in living near the sea, or some other large body of water. This isn't essential to your well-being but it does feed your imagination. The vastness of nature in all its forms probably appeals to you in any case and most Pisceans love the natural world with its staggering diversity.

In love you are ardent and sincere, but you do need to make sure that you choose the right individual to suit you. Pisceans often settle for a protecting arm, but if this turns out to be stifling, trouble could follow. You would find it hard to live with anyone who didn't have at least a degree of your sensitivity, and you need a partner who will allow you to retain that sense of inner freedom that is so vital to your well-being.

Make the most of the many gifts and virtues that nature has bestowed upon you and don't be afraid to let people know what you really are. Actually establishing this in the first place isn't easy for you. Pisceans respond well to almost any form of meditation, which is not surprising because the sign of the Fishes is the most spiritually motivated zodiac sign of them all. When you know yourself fully you generate a personality that is an inspiration to everyone.

PISCES ON THE CUSP

Old Moore is often asked how astrological profiles are altered for those people born at either the beginning or the end of a zodiac sign, or, more properly, on the cusps of a sign. In the case of Pisces this would be on the 20th of February and for two or three days after, and similarly at the end of the sign, probably from the 18th to the 20th of March. In this year's Astral Diaries, once again, Old Moore sets out to explain the differences regarding cuspid signs.

The Aquarius Cusp – February 20th to 22nd

This tends to be a generally happy combination of signs, even if some of the people you come into contact with find you rather difficult to understand from time to time. You are quite capable of cutting a dash, as any Aquarian would be, and yet at the same time you have the quiet and contemplative qualities more typified by Pisces. You tend to be seen as an immensely attractive person, even if you are the last one in the world to accept this fact. People find you to be friendly, very approachable and good company in almost any social or personal setting. It isn't hard for you to get on with others, though since you are not so naturally quiet as Pisces when taken alone, you are slightly more willing to speak your mind and to help out, though usually in a very diplomatic manner.

At work you are very capable and many people with this combination find themselves working on behalf of humanity as a whole. Thus work in social services, hospitals or charities really suits the unique combinations thrown up by this sign mixture. Management is right up your street, though there are times when your conception of popularity takes the foremost place in your mind. Occasionally this could take the edge off executive decisions. A careful attention to detail shows you in a position to get things done, even jobs that others shun. You don't really care for getting your hands dirty but will tackle almost any task if you know it to be necessary. Being basically self-sufficient, you also love the company of others, and it is this adaptability that is the hallmark of success to Aquarian-cusp Pisceans.

Few people actually know you as well as they think they do because the waters of your nature run quite deep. Your real task in life is to let the world know how you feel, something you fight shy of doing now and again. There are positive gains in your life, brought about as a result of your adaptable and pleasing nature. Aquarius present in the nature allows Pisces to act at its best.

The Aries Cusp – March 18th to 20th

This is a Piscean with attitude and probably one of the most difficult zodiac sign combinations to be understood, not only by those people with whom you come into contact but clearly by yourself too. If there are any problems thrown up here they come from the fact that Pisces and Aries have such different ways of expressing themselves to the world at large. Aries is very upfront, dynamic and dominant, all factors that are simply diametrically opposed to the way Pisces thinks and behaves. So the real task in life is to find ways to combine the qualities of Pisces and Aries, in a way that suits the needs of both and without becoming totally confused with regard to your basic nature.

The problem is usually solved by a compartmentation of life. For example, many people with this combination will show the Aries qualities strongly at work, whilst dropping into the Piscean mode socially and at home. This may invariably be the case but there are bound to be times when the underlying motivations become mixed, which can confuse those with whom you come into contact.

Having said all of this you can be the least selfish and most successful individual when you are fighting for the rights of others. This is the zodiac combination of the true social reformer, the genuine politician and the committed pacifist. It seems paradoxical to suggest that someone could fight tenaciously for peace, but this is certainly true in your case. You have excellent executive skills and yet retain an ability to tell other people what they should be doing, in fairly strident terms, usually without upsetting anyone. There is a degree of genuine magic about you that makes you very attractive and there is likely to be more than one love affair in your life. A steadfast view of romance may not be naturally present within your basic nature but like so much else you can 'train' this quality into existence. Personal success is likely, but it probably doesn't matter all that much in a material sense. The important thing to you is being needed by the world at large.

PISCES AND ITS ASCENDANTS

The nature of every individual on the planet is composed of the rich variety of zodiac signs and planetary positions that were present at the time of their birth. Your Sun sign, which in your case is Pisces, is one of the many factors when it comes to assessing the unique person you are. Probably the most important consideration, other than your Sun sign, is to establish the zodiac sign that was rising over the eastern horizon at the time that you were born. This is your Ascending or Rising sign. Most popular astrology fails to take account of the Ascendant, and yet its importance remains with you from the very moment of your birth, through every day of your life. The Ascendant is evident in the way you approach the world, and so, when meeting a person for the first time, it is this astrological influence that you are most likely to notice first. Our Ascending sign essentially represents what we appear to be, while the Sun sign is what we feel inside ourselves.

The Ascendant also has the potential for modifying our overall nature. For example, if you were born at a time of day when Pisces was passing over the eastern horizon (this would be around the time of dawn) then you would be classed as a double Pisces. As such, you would typify this zodiac sign, both internally and in your dealings with others. However, if your Ascendant sign turned out to be a Fire sign, such as Aries, there would be a profound alteration of nature, away from the expected qualities of Pisces.

One of the reasons why popular astrology often ignores the Ascendant is that it has always been rather difficult to establish. Old Moore has found a way to make this possible by devising an easy-to-use table, which you will find on page 158 of this book. Using this, you can establish your Ascendant sign at a glance. You will need to know your rough time of birth, then it is simply a case of following the instructions.

For those readers who have no idea of their time of birth it might be worth allowing a good friend, or perhaps your partner, to read through the section that follows this introduction. Someone who deals with you on a regular basis may easily discover your Ascending sign, even though you could have some difficulty establishing it for yourself. A good understanding of this component of your nature is essential if you want to be aware of that 'other person' who is responsible for the way you make contact with the world at large. Your Sun sign, Ascendant sign, and the other pointers in this book will, together, allow you a far better understanding of what makes you tick as an individual. Peeling back the different layers of your astrological make-up can be an enlightening experience, and the Ascendant may represent one of the most important layers of all.

Pisces with Pisces Ascendant

You are a kind and considerate person who would do almost anything to please the people around you. Creative and extremely perceptive, nobody knows the twists and turns of human nature better than you do, and you make it your business to serve humanity in any way you can. Not everyone understands what makes you tick, and part of the reason for this state of affairs is that you are often not really quite 'in' the world as much as the people you encounter in a day-to-day sense. At work you are generally cheerful, though you can be very quiet on occasions, but since you are consistent in this regard, you don't attract adverse attention or accusations of being moody, as some other variants of Pisces sometimes do. Confusion can beset you on occasions, especially when you are trying to reconcile your own opposing needs. There are certain moments of discontent to be encountered which so often come from trying to please others, even when to do so goes against your own instincts.

As age and experience add to your personal armoury you relax more with the world and find yourself constantly sought out for words of wisdom. The vast majority of people care for you deeply.

Pisces with Aries Ascendant

Although not an easy combination to deal with, the Pisces with an Aries Ascendant does bring something very special to the world in the way of natural understanding allied to practical assistance. It's true that you can sometimes be a dreamer, but there is nothing wrong with that as long as you have the ability to turn some of your wishes into reality, and this you are usually able to do, often for the sake of those around you. Conversation comes easily to you, though you also possess a slightly wistful and poetic side to your nature, which is attractive to the many people who call you a friend. A natural entertainer, you bring a sense of the comic to the often serious qualities of Aries, though without losing the determination that typifies the sign.

In relationships you are ardent, sincere and supportive, with a social conscience that sometimes finds you fighting the battles of the less privileged members of society. Family is important to you and this is a combination that invariably leads to parenthood. Away from the cut and thrust of everyday life you relax more fully, and think about matters more deeply than more typical Aries types might.

Pisces with Taurus Ascendant

You are clearly a very sensitive type of person and that sometimes makes it rather difficult for others to know how they might best approach you. Private and deep, you are nevertheless socially inclined on many occasions. However, because your nature is bottomless it is possible that some types would actually accuse you of being shallow. How can this come about? Well, it's simple really. The fact is that you rarely show anyone what is going on in the deepest recesses of your mind and so your responses can appear to be trite or even ill-considered. This is far from the truth, as those who are allowed into the 'inner sanctum' would readily admit. You are something of a sensualist, and relish staying in bed late and simply pleasing yourself for days on end. However, you have Taurean traits so you desire a tidy environment in which to live your usually long life.

You are able to deal with the routine aspects of life quite well and can be a capable worker once you are up and firing on all cylinders. It is very important that you maintain an interest in what you are doing, because the recesses of your dreamy mind can sometimes appear to be infinitely more attractive. Your imagination is second to none and this fact can often be turned to your advantage.

Pisces with Gemini Ascendant

There is great duality inherent in this combination, and sometimes this can cause a few problems. Part of the trouble stems from the fact that you often fail to realise what you want from life, and you could also be accused of failing to take the time out to think things through carefully enough. You are reactive, and although you have every bit of the natural charm that typifies the sign of Gemini, you are more prone to periods of self-doubt and confusion. However, you should not allow these facts to get you down too much, because you are also genuinely loved and have a tremendous capacity to look after others, a factor which is more important to you than any other. It's true that personal relationships can sometimes be a cause of difficulty for you, partly because your constant need to know what makes other people tick could drive them up the wall. Accepting people at face value seems to be the best key to happiness of a personal sort, and there are occasions when your very real and natural intuition has to be put on hold.

It's likely that you are an original, particularly in the way you dress. An early rebellious stage often gives way to a more comfortable form of eccentricity. When you are at your best, just about everyone adores you.

Pisces with Cancer Ascendant

A deep, double Water-sign combination this, and it might serve to make you a very misunderstood, though undoubtedly popular, individual. You are anxious to make a good impression, probably too keen under certain circumstances, and you do everything you can to help others, even if you don't know them very well. It's true that you are deeply sensitive and quite easily brought to tears by the suffering of this most imperfect world that we inhabit. Fatigue can be a problem, though this is somewhat nullified by the fact that you can withdraw completely into the deep recesses of your own mind when it becomes necessary to do so.

You may not be the most gregarious person in the world, simply because it isn't easy for you to put some of your most important considerations into words. This is easier when you are in the company of people you know and trust, though even trust is a commodity that is difficult for you to find, particularly since you may have been hurt by being too willing to share your thoughts early in life. With age comes wisdom and maturity, and the older you are, the better you will learn to handle this potent and demanding combination. You will never go short of either friends or would-be lovers, and may be one of the most magnetic types of both Cancer and Pisces.

Pisces with Leo Ascendant

You are a very sensitive soul, on occasions too much so for your own good. However, there is not a better advocate for the rights of humanity than you represent and you constantly do what you can to support the downtrodden and oppressed. Good causes are your thing and there are likely to be many in your life. You will probably find yourself pushed to the front of almost any enterprise of which you are a part because, despite the deeper qualities of Pisces, you are a natural leader. Even on those occasions when it feels as though you lack confidence, you manage to muddle through somehow and your smile is as broad as the day. Few sign combinations are more loved than this one, mainly because you do not have a malicious bone in your body, and will readily forgive and forget, which the Lion on its own often will not.

Although you are capable of acting on impulse, you do so from a deep sense of moral conviction, so that most of your endeavours are designed to suit other people too. They recognise this fact and will push much support back in your direction. Even when you come across troubles in your life you manage to find ways to sort them out, and will invariably notice something new to smile about on the way. Your sensitivity rating is massive and you can easily be moved to tears.

Pisces with Virgo Ascendant

You might have been accused on occasions of being too sensitive for your own good, a charge that is not entirely without foundation. Certainly you are very understanding of the needs of others, sometimes to the extent that you put everything aside to help them. This would also be true in the case of charities, for you care very much about the world and the people who cling tenaciously to its surface. Your ability to love on a one-to-one basis knows no bounds, though you may not discriminate as much as you could, particularly when young, and might have one or two false starts in the love stakes. You don't always choose to verbalise your thoughts and this can cause problems, because there is always so much going on in your mind and Virgo especially needs good powers of communication. Pisces is quieter and you need to force yourself to say what you think when the explanation is important.

You would never betray a confidence and sometimes take on rather more for the sake of your friends than is strictly good for you. This is not a fault but can cause you problems all the same. Because you are so intuitive there is little that escapes your attention, though you should avoid being pessimistic about your insights. Changes of scenery suit you and travel would bring out the best in what can be a repressed nature.

Pisces with Libra Ascendant

An Air and Water combination, you are not easy to understand and have depths that show at times, surprising those people who thought they already knew what you were. You will always keep people guessing and are just as likely to hitchhike around Europe as you are to hold down a steady job, both of which you would undertake with the same degree of commitment and success. Usually young at heart, but always carrying the potential for an old head on young shoulders, you are something of a paradox and not at all easy for totally 'straight' types to understand. But you always make an impression, and tend to be very attractive to members of the opposite sex.

In matters of health you do have to be a little careful because you dissipate much nervous energy and can sometimes be inclined to push yourself too hard, at least in a mental sense. Frequent periods of rest and meditation will do you the world of good and should improve your level of wisdom, which tends to be fairly high already. Much of your effort in life is expounded on behalf of humanity as a whole, for you care deeply, love totally and always give of your best. Whatever your faults and failings might be, you are one of the most popular people around.

Pisces with Scorpio Ascendant

You stand a chance of disappearing so deep into yourself that other people would need one of those long ladders that cave explorers use to even find you. It isn't really your fault, because both Scorpio and Pisces, as Water signs, are difficult to understand and you have them both. But that doesn't mean that you should be content to remain in the dark, and the warmth of your nature is all you need to shine a light on the wonderful qualities you possess. But the primary word of warning is that you must put yourself on display and allow others to know what you are, before their appreciation of these facts becomes apparent.

As a server of the world you are second to none and it is hard to find a person with this combination who is not, in some way, looking out for the people around them. Immensely attractive to others, you are also one of the most sought-after lovers. Much of this has to do with your deep and abiding charm, but the air of mystery that surrounds you also helps. Some of you will marry too early, and end up regretting the fact, though the majority of people with Scorpio and Pisces will find the love they deserve in the end. You are able, just, firm but fair, though a sucker for a hard luck story and as kind as the day is long. It's hard to imagine how so many good points could be ignored by others.

Pisces with Sagittarius Ascendant

A very attractive combination this, because the more dominant qualities of the Archer are somehow mellowed-out by the caring Water-sign qualities of the Fishes. You can be very outgoing, but there is always a deeper side to your nature that allows others to know that you are thinking about them. Few people could fall out with either your basic nature or your attitude to the world at large, even though there are depths to your nature that may not be easily understood. You are capable, have a good executive ability and can work hard to achieve your objectives, even if you get a little disillusioned on the way. Much of your life is given over to helping those around you and there is a great tendency for you to work for and on behalf of humanity as a whole. A sense of community is brought to most of what you do and you enjoy co-operation. Although you have the natural ability to attract people to you, the Pisces half of your nature makes you just a little more reserved in personal matters than might otherwise be the case. More careful in your choices than either sign taken alone, you still have to make certain that your motivations when commencing a personal relationship are the right ones. You love to be happy, and to offer gifts of happiness to others.

Pisces with Capricorn Ascendant

You are certainly not the easiest person in the world to understand, mainly because your nature is so deep and your personality so complicated, that others are somewhat intimidated at the prospect of staring into this abyss. All the same your friendly nature is attractive, and there will always be people around who are fascinated by the sheer magnetic quality that is intrinsic to this zodiac mix. Sentimental and extremely kind, there is no limit to the extent of your efforts on behalf of a deserving world, though there are some people around who wonder at your commitment and who may ridicule you a little for your staying-power, even in the face of some adversity. At work you are very capable, will work long and hard, and can definitely expect a greater degree of financial and practical success than Pisces when taken alone. Routines don't bother you too much, though you do need regular periods of introspection, which help to recharge low batteries and a battered self-esteem. In affairs of the heart you are given to impulse, which belies the more careful qualities of Capricorn. However, the determination remains intact and you are quite capable of chasing rainbows round and round the same field, never realising that you can't get to the end of them. Generally speaking you are an immensely lovable person and a great favourite to many.

Pisces with Aquarius Ascendant

Here we find the originality of Aquarius balanced by the very sensitive qualities of Pisces, and it makes for a very interesting combination. When it comes to understanding other people you are second to none, but it's certain that you are more instinctive than either Pisces or Aquarius when taken alone. You are better at routines than Aquarius, but also relish a challenge more than the typical Piscean would. Active and enterprising, you tend to know what you want from life, but consideration of others, and the world at large, will always be part of the scenario. People with this combination often work on behalf of humanity and are to be found in social work, the medical profession and religious institutions. As far as beliefs are concerned you don't conform to established patterns, and yet may get closer to the truth of the Creator than many deep theological thinkers have ever been able to do. Acting on impulse as much as you do means that not everyone understands the way your mind works, but your popularity will invariably see you through.

Passionate and deeply sensitive, you are able to negotiate the twists and turns of a romantic life that is hardly likely to be run-of-the-mill. In the end, however, you should certainly be able to find a very deep personal and spiritual happiness.

THE MOON AND THE PART IT PLAYS IN YOUR LIFE

In astrology the Moon is probably the single most important heavenly body after the Sun. Its unique position, as partner to the Earth on its journey around the solar system, means that the Moon appears to pass through the signs of the zodiac extremely quickly. The zodiac position of the Moon at the time of your birth plays a great part in personal character and is especially significant in the build-up of your emotional nature.

Sun Moon Cycles

The first lunar cycle deals with the part the position of the Moon plays relative to your Sun sign. I have made the fluctuations of this pattern easy for you to understand by means of a simple cyclic graph. It appears on the first page of each 'Your Month At A Glance', under the title 'Highs and Lows'. The graph displays the lunar cycle and you will soon learn to understand how its movements have a bearing on your level of energy and your abilities.

Your Own Moon Sign

Discovering the position of the Moon at the time of your birth has always been notoriously difficult because tracking the complex zodiac positions of the Moon is not easy. This process has been reduced to three simple stages with Old Moore's unique Lunar Tables. A breakdown of the Moon's zodiac positions can be found from page 25 onwards, so that once you know what your Moon Sign is, you can see what part this plays in the overall build-up of your personal character.

If you follow the instructions on the next page you will soon be able to work out exactly what zodiac sign the Moon occupied on the day that you were born and you can then go on to compare the reading for this position with those of your Sun sign and your Ascendant. It is partly the comparison between these three important positions that goes towards making you the unique individual you are.

HOW TO DISCOVER YOUR MOON SIGN

This is a three-stage process. You may need a pen and a piece of paper but if you follow the instructions below the process should only take a minute or so.

STAGE 1 First of all you need to know the Moon Age at the time of your birth. If you look at Moon Table 1, on page 23, you will find all the years between 1915 and 2013 down the left side. Find the year of your birth and then trace across to the right to the month of your birth. Where the two intersect you will find a number. This is the date of the New Moon in the month that you were born. You now need to count forward the number of days between the New Moon and your own birthday. For example, if the New Moon in the month of your birth was shown as being the 6th and you were born on the 20th, your Moon Age Day would be 14. If the New Moon in the month of your birth came after your birthday, you need to count forward from the New Moon in the previous month. Whatever the result, jot this number down so that you do not forget it.

STAGE 2 Take a look at Moon Table 2 on page 24. Down the left hand column look for the date of your birth. Now trace across to the month of your birth. Where the two meet you will find a letter. Copy this letter down alongside your Moon Age Day.

STAGE 3 Moon Table 3 on page 24 will supply you with the zodiac sign the Moon occupied on the day of your birth. Look for your Moon Age Day down the left hand column and then for the letter you found in Stage 2. Where the two converge you will find a zodiac sign and this is the sign occupied by the Moon on the day that you were born.

Your Zodiac Moon Sign Explained

You will find a profile of all zodiac Moon Signs on pages 25 to 28, showing in yet another way how astrology helps to make you into the individual that you are. In each daily entry of the Astral Diary you can find the zodiac position of the Moon for every day of the year. This also allows you to discover your lunar birthdays. Since the Moon passes through all the signs of the zodiac in about a month, you can expect something like twelve lunar birthdays each year. At these times you are likely to be emotionally steady and able to make the sort of decisions that have real, lasting value.

MOON TABLE 1

YEAR	JAN	FEB	MAR	YEAR	JAN	FEB	MAR	YEAR	JAN	FEB	MAR
1915	15	15	14	1948	11	9	11	1981	6	4	6
1916	5	3	5	1949	29	27	29	1982	25	23	24
1917	24	22	23	1950	18	16	18	1983	14	13	14
1918	12	11	12	1951	7	6	7	1984	3	1	2
1919	1/31	–	2/31	1952	26	25	25	1985	21	19	21
1920	21	19	20	1953	15	14	15	1986	10	9	10
1921	9	8	9	1954	5	3	5	1987	29	28	29
1922	27	26	28	1955	24	22	24	1988	18	17	18
1923	17	15	17	1956	13	11	12	1989	7	6	7
1924	6	5	5	1957	1/30	–	1/31	1990	26	25	26
1925	24	23	24	1958	19	18	20	1991	15	14	15
1926	14	12	14	1959	9	7	9	1992	4	3	4
1927	3	2	3	1960	27	26	27	1993	24	22	24
1928	21	19	21	1961	16	15	16	1994	11	10	12
1929	11	9	11	1962	6	5	6	1995	1/31	–	1/30
1930	29	28	30	1963	25	23	25	1996	19	18	19
1931	18	17	19	1964	14	13	14	1997	9	7	9
1932	7	6	7	1965	3	1	2	1998	27	26	27
1933	25	24	26	1966	21	19	21	1999	16	15	16
1934	15	14	15	1967	10	9	10	2000	6	4	6
1935	5	3	5	1968	29	28	29	2001	24	23	25
1936	24	22	23	1969	19	17	18	2002	13	12	13
1937	12	11	12	1970	7	6	7	2003	3	1	2
1938	1/31	–	2/31	1971	26	25	26	2004	21	20	21
1939	20	19	20	1972	15	14	15	2005	10	9	10
1940	9	8	9	1973	5	4	5	2006	29	28	29
1941	27	26	27	1974	24	22	24	2007	18	16	18
1942	16	15	16	1975	12	11	12	2008	8	6	7
1943	6	4	6	1976	1/31	29	30	2009	26	25	26
1944	25	24	24	1977	19	18	19	2010	15	14	15
1945	14	12	14	1978	9	7	9	2011	4	3	5
1946	3	2	3	1979	27	26	27	2012	23	22	22
1947	21	19	21	1980	16	15	16	2013	12	10	12

TABLE 2

DAY	FEB	MAR
1	D	F
2	D	G
3	D	G
4	D	G
5	D	G
6	D	G
7	D	G
8	D	G
9	D	G
10	E	G
11	E	G
12	E	H
13	E	H
14	E	H
15	E	H
16	E	H
17	E	H
18	E	H
19	E	H
20	F	H
21	F	H
22	F	I
23	F	I
24	F	I
25	F	I
26	F	I
27	F	I
28	F	I
29	F	I
30	–	I
31	–	I

TABLE 3

M/D	D	E	F	G	H	I	J
0	AQ	PI	PI	PI	AR	AR	AR
1	PI	PI	PI	AR	AR	AR	TA
2	PI	PI	AR	AR	AR	TA	TA
3	PI	AR	AR	AR	TA	TA	TA
4	AR	AR	AR	TA	TA	GE	GE
5	AR	TA	TA	TA	GE	GE	GE
6	TA	TA	TA	GE	GE	GE	CA
7	TA	TA	GE	GE	GE	CA	CA
8	TA	GE	GE	GE	CA	CA	CA
9	GE	GE	CA	CA	CA	CA	LE
10	GE	CA	CA	CA	LE	LE	LE
11	CA	CA	CA	LE	LE	LE	VI
12	CA	CA	LE	LE	LE	VI	VI
13	LE	LE	LE	LE	VI	VI	VI
14	LE	LE	VI	VI	VI	LI	LI
15	LE	VI	VI	VI	LI	LI	LI
16	VI	VI	VI	LI	LI	LI	SC
17	VI	VI	LI	LI	LI	SC	SC
18	VI	LI	LI	LI	SC	SC	SC
19	LI	LI	LI	SC	SC	SC	SA
20	LI	SC	SC	SC	SA	SA	SA
21	SC	SC	SC	SA	SA	SA	CP
22	SC	SC	SA	SA	SA	CP	CP
23	SC	SA	SA	SA	CP	CP	CP
24	SA	SA	SA	CP	CP	CP	AQ
25	SA	CP	CP	CP	AQ	AQ	AQ
26	CP	CP	CP	AQ	AQ	AQ	PI
27	CP	AQ	AQ	AQ	AQ	PI	PI
28	AQ	AQ	AQ	AQ	PI	PI	PI
29	AQ	AQ	AQ	PI	PI	PI	AR

AR = Aries, TA = Taurus, GE = Gemini, CA = Cancer, LE = Leo, VI = Virgo, LI = Libra, SC = Scorpio, SA = Sagittarius, CP = Capricorn, AQ = Aquarius, PI = Pisces

MOON SIGNS

Moon in Aries

You have a strong imagination, courage, determination and a desire to do things in your own way and forge your own path through life.

Originality is a key attribute; you are seldom stuck for ideas although your mind is changeable and you could take the time to focus on individual tasks. Often quick-tempered, you take orders from few people and live life at a fast pace. Avoid health problems by taking regular time out for rest and relaxation.

Emotionally, it is important that you talk to those you are closest to and work out your true feelings. Once you discover that people are there to help, there is less necessity for you to do everything yourself.

Moon in Taurus

The Moon in Taurus gives you a courteous and friendly manner, which means you are likely to have many friends.

The good things in life mean a lot to you, as Taurus is an Earth sign that delights in experiences which please the senses. Hence you are probably a lover of good food and drink, which may in turn mean you need to keep an eye on the bathroom scales, especially as looking good is also important to you.

Emotionally you are fairly stable and you stick by your own standards. Taureans do not respond well to change. Intuition also plays an important part in your life.

Moon in Gemini

You have a warm-hearted character, sympathetic and eager to help others. At times reserved, you can also be articulate and chatty: this is part of the paradox of Gemini, which always brings duplicity to the nature. You are interested in current affairs, have a good intellect, and are good company and likely to have many friends. Most of your friends have a high opinion of you and would be ready to defend you should the need arise. However, this is usually unnecessary, as you are quite capable of defending yourself in any verbal confrontation.

Travel is important to your inquisitive mind and you find intellectual stimulus in mixing with people from different cultures. You also gain much from reading, writing and the arts but you do need plenty of rest and relaxation in order to avoid fatigue.

Moon in Cancer

The Moon in Cancer at the time of birth is a fortunate position as Cancer is the Moon's natural home. This means that the qualities of compassion and understanding given by the Moon are especially enhanced in your nature, and you are friendly and sociable and cope well with emotional pressures. You cherish home and family life, and happily do the domestic tasks. Your surroundings are important to you and you hate squalor and filth. You are likely to have a love of music and poetry.

Your basic character, although at times changeable like the Moon itself, depends on symmetry. You aim to make your surroundings comfortable and harmonious, for yourself and those close to you.

Moon in Leo

The best qualities of the Moon and Leo come together to make you warmhearted, fair, ambitious and self-confident. With good organisational abilities, you invariably rise to a position of responsibility in your chosen career. This is fortunate as you don't enjoy being an 'also-ran' and would rather be an important part of a small organisation than a menial in a large one.

You should be lucky in love, and happy, provided you put in the effort to make a comfortable home for yourself and those close to you. It is likely that you will have a love of pleasure, sport, music and literature. Life brings you many rewards, most of them as a direct result of your own efforts, although you may be luckier than average and ready to make the best of any situation.

Moon in Virgo

You are endowed with good mental abilities and a keen receptive memory, but you are never ostentatious or pretentious. Naturally quite reserved, you still have many friends, especially of the opposite sex. Marital relationships must be discussed carefully and worked at so that they remain harmonious, as personal attachments can be a problem if you do not give them your full attention.

Talented and persevering, you possess artistic qualities and are a good homemaker. Earning your honours through genuine merit, you work long and hard towards your objectives but show little pride in your achievements. Many short journeys will be undertaken in your life.

Moon in Libra

With the Moon in Libra you are naturally popular and make friends easily. People like you, probably more than you realise, you bring fun to a party and are a natural diplomat. For all its good points, Libra is not the most stable of astrological signs and, as a result, your emotions can be a little unstable too. Therefore, although the Moon in Libra is said to be good for love and marriage, your Sun sign and Rising sign will have an important effect on your emotional and loving qualities.

You must remember to relate to others in your decision-making. Co-operation is crucial because Libra represents the 'balance' of life that can only be achieved through harmonious relationships. Conformity is not easy for you because Libra, an Air sign, likes its independence.

Moon in Scorpio

Some people might call you pushy. In fact, all you really want to do is to live life to the full and protect yourself and your family from the pressures of life. Take care to avoid giving the impression of being sarcastic or impulsive and use your energies wisely and constructively.

You have great courage and you invariably achieve your goals by force of personality and sheer effort. You are fond of mystery and are good at predicting the outcome of situations and events. Travel experiences can be beneficial to you.

You may experience problems if you do not take time to examine your motives in a relationship, and also if you allow jealousy, always a feature of Scorpio, to cloud your judgement.

Moon in Sagittarius

The Moon in Sagittarius helps to make you a generous individual with humanitarian qualities and a kind heart. Restlessness may be intrinsic as your mind is seldom still. Perhaps because of this, you have a need for change that could lead you to several major moves during your adult life. You are not afraid to stand your ground when you know your judgement is right, you speak directly and have good intuition.

At work you are quick, efficient and versatile and so you make an ideal employee. You need work to be intellectually demanding and do not enjoy tedious routines.

In relationships, you anger quickly if faced with stupidity or deception, though you are just as quick to forgive and forget. Emotionally, there are times when your heart rules your head.

Moon in Capricorn

The Moon in Capricorn makes you popular and likely to come into the public eye in some way. The watery Moon is not entirely comfortable in the Earth sign of Capricorn and this may lead to some difficulties in the early years of life. An initial lack of creative ability and indecision must be overcome before the true qualities of patience and perseverance inherent in Capricorn can show through.

You have good administrative ability and are a capable worker, and if you are careful you can accumulate wealth. But you must be cautious and take professional advice in partnerships, as you are open to deception. You may be interested in social or welfare work, which suit your organisational skills and sympathy for others.

Moon in Aquarius

The Moon in Aquarius makes you an active and agreeable person with a friendly, easy-going nature. Sympathetic to the needs of others, you flourish in a laid-back atmosphere. You are broad-minded, fair and open to suggestion, although sometimes you have an unconventional quality which others can find hard to understand.

You are interested in the strange and curious, and in old articles and places. You enjoy trips to these places and gain much from them. Political, scientific and educational work interests you and you might choose a career in science or technology.

Money-wise, you make gains through innovation and concentration and Lunar Aquarians often tackle more than one job at a time. In love you are kind and honest.

Moon in Pisces

You have a kind, sympathetic nature, somewhat retiring at times, but you always take account of others' feelings and help when you can.

Personal relationships may be problematic, but as life goes on you can learn from your experiences and develop a better understanding of yourself and the world around you.

You have a fondness for travel, appreciate beauty and harmony and hate disorder and strife. You may be fond of literature and would make a good writer or speaker yourself. You have a creative imagination and may come across as an incurable romantic. You have strong intuition, maybe bordering on a mediumistic quality, which sets you apart from the mass. You may not be rich in cash terms, but your personal gifts are worth more than gold.

PISCES IN LOVE

Discover how compatible in love you are with people from the same and other signs of the zodiac. Five stars equals a match made in heaven!

Pisces meets Pisces

Pisceans are easy-going and get on well with most people, so when two Pisceans get together, harmony is invariably the result. While this isn't the most dynamic relationship, there is mutual understanding, and a desire to please on both sides. Neither partner is likely to be overbearing or selfish. Family responsibilities should be happily shared and home surroundings will be comfortable, but never pretentious. One of the better pairings for the sign of the Fishes. Star rating: *****

Pisces meets Aries

Still waters run deep, and they don't come much deeper than Pisces. Although these signs share the same quadrant of the zodiac, they have little in common. Pisces is a dreamer, a romantic idealist with steady and spiritual goals. Aries needs to be on the move, and has very different ideals. It's hard to see how a relationship could develop but, with patience, there is a chance that things might work out. Pisces needs incentive, and Aries may be the sign to offer it. Star rating: **

Pisces meets Taurus

No problem here, unless both parties come from the quieter side of their respective signs. Most of the time Taurus and Pisces would live comfortably together, offering mutual support and deep regard. Taurus can offer the personal qualities that Pisces craves, whilst Pisces understands and copes with the Bull's slightly stubborn qualities. Taurus is likely to travel in Piscean company, so there is a potential for wide-ranging experiences and variety which is essential. There will be some misunderstandings, mainly because Pisces is so deep, but that won't prevent their enduring happiness. Star rating: ***

Pisces meets Gemini

Gemini likes to think of itself as intuitive and intellectual, but it will never understand Pisces' dark depths. Another stumbling block is that both Gemini and Pisces are 'split' signs – the Twins and the two Fishes – which means that both are capable of dual personalities. There won't be any shortage of affection, but the real question has to be how much these people feel they have in common. Pisces is extremely kind, and so is Gemini most of the time. But Pisces does too much soul-searching for Gemini, who might eventually become bored. Star rating: ***

Pisces meets Cancer

This is likely to be a very successful match. Cancer and Pisces are both Water signs, both deep, sensitive and very caring. Pisces loves deeply, and Cancer wants to be loved. There will be few fireworks here, and a very quiet house. But that doesn't mean that either love or action is lacking – the latter of which is just behind closed doors. Family and children are important to both signs and both are prepared to work hard, but Pisces is the more restless of the two and needs the support and security that Cancer offers. Star rating: *****

Pisces meets Leo

Pisces always needs to understand others, which makes Leo feel warm and loved, while Leo sees, to its delight, that Pisces needs to be protected and taken care of. Pisceans are often lacking in self-confidence which is something Leo has to spare, and happily it is often infectious. Pisces' inevitable cares are swept away on a tide of Leonine cheerfulness. This couple's home would be cheerful and full of love, which is beneficial to all family members. This is not a meeting of minds, but rather an understanding and appreciation of differences. Star rating: ****

Pisces meets Virgo

This looks an unpromising match from beginning to end. There are exceptions to every rule, particularly where Pisces is concerned, but these two signs are both so deep it's hard to imagine that they could ever find what makes the other tick. The depth is different in each case: Virgo's ruminations are extremely materialistic, while Pisces exists in a world of deep-felt, poorly expressed emotion. Pisces and Virgo might find they don't talk much, so only in a contemplative, almost monastic, match would they ever get on. Still, in a vast zodiac, anything is possible. Star rating: **

Pisces meets Libra

Libra and Pisces can be extremely fond of each other, even deeply in love, but this alone isn't a stable foundation for long-term success. Pisces is extremely deep and doesn't even know itself very well. Libra may initially find this intriguing but will eventually feel frustrated at being unable to understand the Piscean's emotional and personal feelings. Pisces can be jealous and may find Libra's flightiness difficult, which Libra can't stand. They are great friends and they may make it to the romantic stakes, but when they get there a great deal of effort will be necessary. Star rating: ***

Pisces meets Scorpio

If ever there were two zodiac signs that have a total rapport, it has to be Scorpio and Pisces. They share very similar needs: they are not gregarious and are happy with a little silence, good music and time to contemplate the finer things in life, and both are attracted to family life. Apart, they can have a tendency to wander in a romantic sense, but this is reduced when they come together. They are deep, firm friends who enjoy each other's company and this must lead to an excellent chance of success. These people are surely made for each other! Star rating: *****

Pisces meets Sagittarius

Probably the least likely success story for either sign, which is why it scores so low on the star rating. The basic problem is an almost total lack of understanding. A successful relationship needs empathy and progress towards a shared goal but, although both are eager to please, Pisces is too deep and Sagittarius too flighty – they just don't belong on the same planet! As pals, they have more in common and so a friendship is the best hope of success and happiness. Star rating: *

Pisces meets Capricorn

There is some chance of a happy relationship here, but it will need work on both sides. Capricorn is a go-getter, but likes to plan long term. Pisces is naturally more immediate, but has enough intuition to understand the Goat's thinking. Both have patience, but it will usually be Pisces who chooses to play second fiddle. The quiet nature of both signs might be a problem, as someone will have to take the lead, especially in social situations. Both signs should recognise this fact and accommodate it. Star rating: ***

Pisces meets Aquarius

Zodiac signs that follow each other often have something in common, but this is often not the case with Aquarius and Pisces. Both signs are deeply caring, but in different ways. Pisces is one of the deepest zodiac signs, and Aquarius simply isn't prepared to embark on the journey. Pisceans, meanwhile, would probably find Aquarians superficial and even flippant. On the positive side, there is potential for a well-balanced relationship, but unless one party is untypical of their zodiac sign, it often doesn't get started. Star rating: **

VENUS:
THE PLANET OF LOVE

If you look up at the sky around sunset or sunrise you will often see Venus in close attendance to the Sun. It is arguably one of the most beautiful sights of all and there is little wonder that historically it became associated with the goddess of love. But although Venus does play an important part in the way you view love and in the way others see you romantically, this is only one of the spheres of influence that it enjoys in your overall character.

Venus has a part to play in the more cultured side of your life and has much to do with your appreciation of art, literature, music and general creativity. Even the way you look is responsive to the part of the zodiac that Venus occupied at the start of your life, though this fact is also down to your Sun sign and Ascending sign. If, at the time you were born, Venus occupied one of the more gregarious zodiac signs, you will be more likely to wear your heart on your sleeve, as well as to be more attracted to entertainment, social gatherings and good company. If on the other hand Venus occupied a quiet zodiac sign at the time of your birth, you would tend to be more retiring and less willing to shine in public situations.

It's good to know what part the planet Venus plays in your life for it can have a great bearing on the way you appear to the rest of the world and since we all have to mix with others, you can learn to make the very best of what Venus has to offer you.

One of the great complications in the past has always been trying to establish exactly what zodiac position Venus enjoyed when you were born because the planet is notoriously difficult to track. However, I have solved that problem by creating a table that is exclusive to your Sun sign, which you will find on the following page.

Establishing your Venus sign could not be easier. Just look up the year of your birth on the page opposite and you will see a sign of the zodiac. This was the sign that Venus occupied in the period covered by your sign in that year. If Venus occupied more than one sign during the period, this is indicated by the date on which the sign changed, and the name of the new sign. For instance, if you were born in 1940, Venus was in Aries until the 9th March, after which time it was in Taurus. If you were born before 9th March your Venus sign is Aries, if you were born on or after 9th March, your Venus sign is Taurus. Once you have established the position of Venus at the time of your birth, you can then look in the pages which follow to see how this has a bearing on your life as a whole.

1915 CAPRICORN
1916 ARIES / 10.3 TAURUS
1917 AQUARIUS / 5.3 PISCES
1918 AQUARIUS
1919 PISCES / 27.2 ARIES
1920 CAPRICORN /
    24.2 AQUARIUS / 19.3 PISCES
1921 ARIES / 8.3 TAURUS
1922 PISCES / 14.3 ARIES
1923 CAPRICORN
1924 ARIES / 10.3 TAURUS
1925 AQUARIUS / 4.3 PISCES
1926 AQUARIUS
1927 PISCES / 26.2 ARIES
1928 CAPRICORN /
    23.2 AQUARIUS / 18.3 PISCES
1929 ARIES / 9.3 TAURUS
1930 PISCES / 13.3 ARIES
1931 CAPRICORN
1932 ARIES / 9.3 TAURUS
1933 AQUARIUS / 4.3 PISCES
1934 AQUARIUS
1935 PISCES / 25.2 ARIES
1936 CAPRICORN /
    23.2 AQUARIUS / 18.3 PISCES
1937 ARIES / 10.3 TAURUS
1938 PISCES / 12.3 ARIES
1939 CAPRICORN
1940 ARIES / 9.3 TAURUS
1941 AQUARIUS / 3.3 PISCES
1942 AQUARIUS
1943 PISCES / 25.2 ARIES
1944 CAPRICORN /
    22.2 AQUARIUS / 18.3 PISCES
1945 ARIES / 11.3 TAURUS
1946 PISCES / 11.3 ARIES
1947 CAPRICORN
1948 ARIES / 8.3 TAURUS
1949 AQUARIUS / 3.3 PISCES
1950 AQUARIUS
1951 PISCES / 24.2 ARIES
1952 CAPRICORN /
    22.2 AQUARIUS / 17.3 PISCES
1953 ARIES
1954 PISCES / 11.3 ARIES
1955 CAPRICORN
1956 ARIES / 8.3 TAURUS
1957 AQUARIUS / 2.3 PISCES
1958 CAPRICORN /
    25.2 AQUARIUS
1959 PISCES / 24.2 ARIES
1960 CAPRICORN /
    21.2 AQUARIUS / 17.3 PISCES
1961 ARIES
1962 PISCES / 10.3 ARIES
1963 CAPRICORN
1964 ARIES / 8.3 TAURUS

1965 AQUARIUS / 1.3 PISCES
1966 AQUARIUS
1967 PISCES / 23.2 ARIES
1968 SAGITTARIUS /
    26.1 CAPRICORN
1969 ARIES
1970 PISCES / 10.3 ARIES
1971 CAPRICORN
1972 ARIES / 7.3 TAURUS
1973 AQUARIUS / 1.3 PISCES
1974 CAPRICORN / 2.3 AQUARIUS
1975 PISCES / 23.2 ARIES
1976 SAGITTARIUS /
    26.1 CAPRICORN
1977 ARIES
1978 PISCES / 9.3 ARIES
1979 CAPRICORN
1980 ARIES / 7.3 TAURUS
1981 AQUARIUS / 28.2 PISCES
1982 CAPRICORN / 4.3 AQUARIUS
1983 PISCES / 23.2 ARIES
1984 SAGITTARIUS /
    25.1 CAPRICORN
1985 ARIES
1986 PISCES / 9.3 ARIES
1987 CAPRICORN
1988 ARIES / 7.3 TAURUS
1989 AQUARIUS / 28.2 PISCES
1990 CAPRICORN / 5.3 AQUARIUS
1991 PISCES / 22.2 ARIES /
    20.3 TAURUS
1992 SAGITTARIUS /
    25.1 CAPRICORN
1993 ARIES
1994 PISCES / 9.3 ARIES
1995 CAPRICORN
1996 ARIES / 7.3 TAURUS
1997 AQUARIUS / 27.2 PISCES
1998 CAPRICORN / 5.3 AQUARIUS
1999 PISCES / 22.2 ARIES /
    19.3 TAURUS
2000 SAGITTARIUS /
    25.1 CAPRICORN
2001 ARIES
2002 PISCES / 9.3 ARIES
2003 CAPRICORN
2004 ARIES / 7.3 TAURUS
2005 AQUARIUS / 27.2 PISCES
2006 CAPRICORN / 5.3 AQUARIUS
2007 PISCES / 22.2 ARIES
2008 SAGITTARIUS /
    25.1 CAPRICORN
2009 ARIES
2010 PISCES / 9.3 ARIES
2011 CAPRICORN
2012 ARIES / 7.3 TAURUS
2013 AQUARIUS / 27.2 PISCES

33

VENUS THROUGH THE ZODIAC SIGNS

Venus in Aries

Amongst other things, the position of Venus in Aries indicates a fondness for travel, music and all creative pursuits. Your nature tends to be affectionate and you would try not to create confusion or difficulty for others if it could be avoided. Many people with this planetary position have a great love of the theatre, and mental stimulation is of the greatest importance. Early romantic attachments are common with Venus in Aries, so it is very important to establish a genuine sense of romantic continuity. Early marriage is not recommended, especially if it is based on sympathy. You may give your heart a little too readily on occasions.

Venus in Taurus

You are capable of very deep feelings and your emotions tend to last for a very long time. This makes you a trusting partner and lover, whose constancy is second to none. In life you are precise and careful and always try to do things the right way. Although this means an ordered life, which you are comfortable with, it can also lead you to be rather too fussy for your own good. Despite your pleasant nature, you are very fixed in your opinions and quite able to speak your mind. Others are attracted to you and historical astrologers always quoted this position of Venus as being very fortunate in terms of marriage. However, if you find yourself involved in a failed relationship, it could take you a long time to trust again.

Venus in Gemini

As with all associations related to Gemini, you tend to be quite versatile, anxious for change and intelligent in your dealings with the world at large. You may gain money from more than one source but you are equally good at spending it. There is an inference here that you are a good communicator, via either the written or the spoken word, and you love to be in the company of interesting people. Always on the look-out for culture, you may also be very fond of music, and love to indulge the curious and cultured side of your nature. In romance you tend to have more than one relationship and could find yourself associated with someone who has previously been a friend or even a distant relative.

Venus in Cancer

You often stay close to home because you are very fond of family and enjoy many of your most treasured moments when you are with those you love. Being naturally sympathetic, you will always do anything you can to support those around you, even people you hardly know at all. This charitable side of your nature is your most noticeable trait and is one of the reasons why others are naturally so fond of you. Being receptive and in some cases even psychic, you can see through to the soul of most of those with whom you come into contact. You may not commence too many romantic attachments but when you do give your heart, it tends to be unconditionally.

Venus in Leo

It must become quickly obvious to almost anyone you meet that you are kind, sympathetic and yet determined enough to stand up for anyone or anything that is truly important to you. Bright and sunny, you warm the world with your natural enthusiasm and would rarely do anything to hurt those around you, or at least not intentionally. In romance you are ardent and sincere, though some may find your style just a little overpowering. Gains come through your contacts with other people and this could be especially true with regard to romance, for love and money often come hand in hand for those who were born with Venus in Leo. People claim to understand you, though you are more complex than you seem.

Venus in Virgo

Your nature could well be fairly quiet no matter what your Sun sign might be, though this fact often manifests itself as an inner peace and would not prevent you from being basically sociable. Some delays and even the odd disappointment in love cannot be ruled out with this planetary position, though it's a fact that you will usually find the happiness you look for in the end. Catapulting yourself into romantic entanglements that you know to be rather ill-advised is not sensible, and it would be better to wait before you committed yourself exclusively to any one person. It is the essence of your nature to serve the world at large and through doing so it is possible that you will attract money at some stage in your life.

Venus in Libra

Venus is very comfortable in Libra and bestows upon those people who have this planetary position a particular sort of kindness that is easy to recognise. This is a very good position for all sorts of friendships and also for romantic attachments that usually bring much joy into your life. Few individuals with Venus in Libra would avoid marriage and since you are capable of great depths of love, it is likely that you will find a contented personal life. You like to mix with people of integrity and intelligence but don't take kindly to scruffy surroundings or work that means getting your hands too dirty. Careful speculation, good business dealings and money through marriage all seem fairly likely.

Venus in Scorpio

You are quite open and tend to spend money quite freely, even on those occasions when you don't have very much. Although your intentions are always good, there are times when you get yourself in to the odd scrape and this can be particularly true when it comes to romance, which you may come to late or from a rather unexpected direction. Certainly you have the power to be happy and to make others contented on the way, but you find the odd stumbling block on your journey through life and it could seem that you have to work harder than those around you. As a result of this, you gain a much deeper understanding of the true value of personal happiness than many people ever do, and are likely to achieve true contentment in the end.

Venus in Sagittarius

You are lighthearted, cheerful and always able to see the funny side of any situation. These facts enhance your popularity, which is especially high with members of the opposite sex. You should never have to look too far to find romantic interest in your life, though it is just possible that you might be too willing to commit yourself before you are certain that the person in question is right for you. Part of the problem here extends to other areas of life too. The fact is that you like variety in everything and so can tire of situations that fail to offer it. All the same, if you choose wisely and learn to understand your restless side, then great happiness can be yours.

Venus in Capricorn

The most notable trait that comes from Venus in this position is that it makes you trustworthy and able to take on all sorts of responsibilities in life. People are instinctively fond of you and love you all the more because you are always ready to help those who are in any form of need. Social and business popularity can be yours and there is a magnetic quality to your nature that is particularly attractive in a romantic sense. Anyone who wants a partner for a lover, a spouse and a good friend too would almost certainly look in your direction. Constancy is the hallmark of your nature and unfaithfulness would go right against the grain. You might sometimes be a little too trusting.

Venus in Aquarius

This location of Venus offers a fondness for travel and a desire to try out something new at every possible opportunity. You are extremely easy to get along with and tend to have many friends from varied backgrounds, classes and inclinations. You like to live a distinct sort of life and gain a great deal from moving about, both in a career sense and with regard to your home. It is not out of the question that you could form a romantic attachment to someone who comes from far away or be attracted to a person of a distinctly artistic and original nature. What you cannot stand is jealousy, for you have friends of both sexes and would want to keep things that way.

Venus in Pisces

The first thing people tend to notice about you is your wonderful, warm smile. Being very charitable by nature you will do anything to help others, even if you don't know them well. Much of your life may be spent sorting out situations for other people, but it is very important to feel that you are living for yourself too. In the main, you remain cheerful, and tend to be quite attractive to members of the opposite sex. Where romantic attachments are concerned, you could be drawn to people who are significantly older or younger than yourself or to someone with a unique career or point of view. It might be best for you to avoid marrying whilst you are still very young.

37

THE ASTRAL DIARY

HOW THE DIAGRAMS WORK

Through the picture diagrams in the Astral Diary I want to help you to plot your year. With them you can see where the positive and negative aspects will be found in each month. To make the most of them, all you have to do is remember where and when!

Let me show you how they work ...

THE MONTH AT A GLANCE

Just as there are twelve separate zodiac signs, so astrologers believe that each sign has twelve separate aspects to life. Each of the twelve segments relates to a different personal aspect. I list them all every month so that their meanings are always clear.

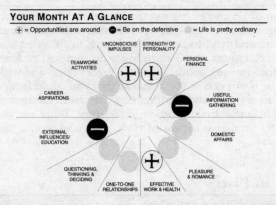

I have designed this chart to show you how and when these twelve different aspects are being influenced throughout the year. When there is a shaded circle, nothing out of the ordinary is to be expected. However, when a circle turns white with a plus sign, the influence is positive. Where the circle is black with a minus sign, it is a negative.

YOUR ENERGY RHYTHM CHART

On the opposite page is a picture diagram in which I link your zodiac group to the rhythm of the Moon. In doing this I have calculated when you will be gaining strength from its influence and equally when you may be weakened by it.

If you think of yourself as being like the tides of the ocean then you may understand how your own energies must also rise and fall. And if you understand how it works and when it is working, then you can better organise your activities to achieve more and get things done more easily.

YOUR ENERGY RHYTHM CHART
At your best on 20th–21st

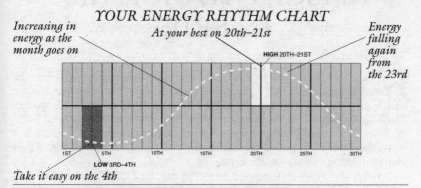

Increasing in energy as the month goes on

HIGH 20TH–21ST

Energy falling again from the 23rd

LOW 3RD–4TH

Take it easy on the 4th

MOVING PICTURE SCREEN
Love, money, career and vitality measured every week

The diagram at the end of each week is designed to be informative and fun. The arrows move up and down the scale to give you an idea of the strength of your opportunities in each area. If LOVE stands at plus 4, then get out and put yourself about because things are going your way in romance! The further down the arrow goes, the weaker the opportunities. Do note that the diagram is an overall view of your astrological aspects and therefore reflects a trend which may not concur with every day in that cycle.

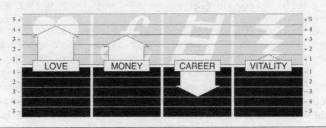

AND FINALLY:

am ....

pm ....

The two lines that are left blank in each daily entry of the Astral Diary are for your own personal use. You may find them ideal for keeping a check on birthdays or appointments, though it could also be an idea to make notes from the astrological trends and diagrams a few weeks in advance. Some of the lines are marked with a key, which indicates the working of astrological cycles in your life. Look out for them each week as they are the best days to take action or make decisions. The daily text tells you which area of your life to focus on.

☿ = Mercury is retrograde on that day.

PISCES: YOUR YEAR IN BRIEF

For various reasons you might not be feeling entirely on top form as the year begins. Don't worry, as trends indicate that this will soon change, and January and February should both work well to your advantage. There are gains to be made in a professional sense, and you should also be able to persuade others to take much greater notice of you than is often the case. Your normal concerns about keeping things in proportion are not even necessary at this time.

March and April might seem to bring quieter trends, but in reality it could simply be that you are being more circumspect. Acting on impulse is now less likely and it pays to cover all your bases at this time. Love could come knocking on your door, especially during March, particularly if you are in a good frame of mind from an emotional point of view. Be careful when it comes to taking any sort of chance financially. You would be better off saving rather than spending.

As summer paints the hedgerows, May and June encourage you to think about all those plans you had at the beginning of the year – a few of which you might now be able to put into action. There is some truth in the old adage: "everything comes to those who wait", and Pisces is certainly no exception to this rule. Now you begin to benefit from the effort you put in earlier in the year and may have cause to be glad of your previous patience.

With July and August comes the opportunity to travel, and this year it is one that you need to grab with both hands. There appears to be no holding you back at this stage and very few people will have the measure of you, either personally or in business. What you say is what you mean and the people around you may be surprised to see such a decisive Piscean.

As the year starts to grow older there could be a few decisions that need making sooner, rather than later. The trouble is that in at least some cases you won't want to make them. September and October represents a time when you need to be decisive and to let yourself and others know that you mean business. Also bear in mind that in a financial and a romantic sense this can be a favourable interlude.

The final two months of the year, November and December, might see you being a little possessive on occasions, something you need to avoid if you can. There is no doubt that you have your thinking head on and you may be able to overcome problems – even those from a long time ago. People come and go in life but new friendships made now tend to endure. The Christmas and New Year period has its quiet moments, but in general you can find happiness and enjoy a positive close to the year.

January

2013

YOUR MONTH AT A GLANCE

⊕ = Opportunities are around ⊖ = Be on the defensive ⬤ = Life is pretty ordinary

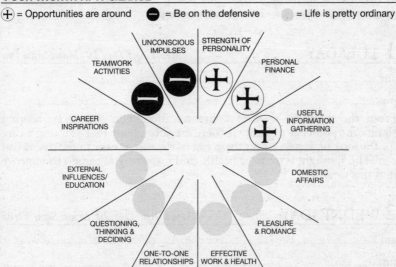

UNCONSCIOUS IMPULSES

STRENGTH OF PERSONALITY

TEAMWORK ACTIVITIES

PERSONAL FINANCE

CAREER INSPIRATIONS

USEFUL INFORMATION GATHERING

EXTERNAL INFLUENCES/ EDUCATION

DOMESTIC AFFAIRS

QUESTIONING, THINKING & DECIDING

PLEASURE & ROMANCE

ONE-TO-ONE RELATIONSHIPS

EFFECTIVE WORK & HEALTH

JANUARY HIGHS AND LOWS

Here I show you how the rhythms of the Moon will affect you this month. Like the tide, your energies and abilities will rise and fall with its pattern. When it is above the centre line, go for it, when it is below, you should be resting.

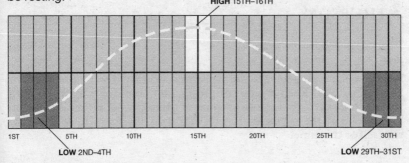

HIGH 15TH–16TH

1ST 5TH 10TH 15TH 20TH 25TH 30TH

LOW 2ND–4TH

LOW 29TH–31ST

31 MONDAY
Moon Age Day 18 Moon Sign Leo

am ....

pm...

The New Year's Eve celebrations are uppermost in your mind and that's fine, though you need to consider practical matters too. Looking ahead, you should be able to create favourable scenarios in certain areas of life. Put your versatile nature to good use today. Flexible and willing to see the greater picture, you can be very good company.

1 TUESDAY
Moon Age Day 19 Moon Sign Leo

am ....

pm...

From the point of view of communication, you should be scoring significant points at present. If there are jobs about that you don't care for the look of, it pays to get them out of the way as early in the day as you can. The spotlight is on your health, and on what you can do to improve it at this time.

2 WEDNESDAY
Moon Age Day 20 Moon Sign Virgo

am ....

pm...

Despite the lunar low, it is towards your career that your mind is encouraged to turn now. Your ability to handle relationships also counts for a great deal, in terms of both avoiding conflict with others and strengthening ties with your partner. Be prepared to investigate the accuracy of information you gather later in the day.

3 THURSDAY
Moon Age Day 21 Moon Sign Virgo

am ....

pm...

Where social arrangements are concerned, you need to be prepared for all eventualities. Keep a sense of proportion, and don't allow yourself to be fazed if you find the behaviour of other people rather difficult to understand at the moment. It won't do you any harm to stick up for yourself at this time.

4 FRIDAY
Moon Age Day 22 Moon Sign Virgo

am..

pm..

There are disruptive influences about, thanks to the continuing presence of the lunar low, but you needn't allow these to have much of a bearing on your life. Today is an ideal opportunity to spend time on your own, doing something you really enjoy. High spirits are possible, though possibly somewhat suppressed now.

5 SATURDAY
Moon Age Day 23 Moon Sign Libra

am..

pm..

Trends indicate just a slight tendency towards a 'know it all' attitude on your part today. This is quite unusual for Pisces, so you could surprise a few people around you. Confidence is a positive attribute, though it's possible to take things too far at present. Pisces is best at humility, which might be hard to find now.

6 SUNDAY
Moon Age Day 24 Moon Sign Libra

am..

pm..

Be prepared to deal with disputes, either in your working life or socially. Your best approach in such cases is simply to withdraw from situations you recognise as being awkward. Causing problems isn't your thing, and you might decide to spend some time on your own, rather than risk contributing to discord.

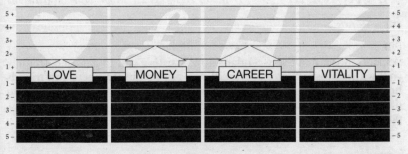

7 MONDAY
Moon Age Day 25 Moon Sign Scorpio

am ....

pm ....

Falling in line with the opinions of people you trust can bring certain advantages now, and you might even be listening to what strangers have to say. Your kind disposition should be clear for all to see, particularly if you put it to good use in helping anyone who is having problems. It's a big part of the Pisces nature.

8 TUESDAY
Moon Age Day 26 Moon Sign Scorpio

am ....

pm ....

Trends today prove to be quite a contrast to yesterday. Even if your aims and objectives are on target, for a few hours at least it may be difficult for you to follow through. Don't worry – these trends certainly won't last long. Focus on keeping busy socially, which probably matters more to you than success just now.

9 WEDNESDAY
Moon Age Day 27 Moon Sign Sagittarius

am ....

pm ....

By all means take time off from certain obligations if you feel you should. However, whatever you decide to do today, you need to choose your own path and show certainty in the actions you are taking. Use the confidence that is available, and as the week wears on, demonstrate that you are working towards one or two triumphs.

10 THURSDAY
Moon Age Day 28 Moon Sign Sagittarius

am ....

pm ....

Social trends are in the ascendant now, assisting you to get on extremely well with almost everyone. Even if you put family members and friends first in your life, you should still be able to find time for people you don't know so well. There's nothing wrong with pursuing a hectic personal schedule!

11 FRIDAY

Moon Age Day 29 Moon Sign Capricorn

am..

pm..

Dealing with slightly taxing situations could well take up at least part of your time today, though you should still be willing to find some fun. Sociability is your middle name, and the competitive side of your nature is also highlighted around now. Use this to your advantage by showing that you won't be beaten at anything.

12 SATURDAY

Moon Age Day 0 Moon Sign Capricorn

am..

pm..

Once again your competitive instincts are promoted this weekend. It's time to decide what you want from life, and think about how you can go about getting it. Social impulses are also well accented, and there is no reason to be tardy when it comes to mixing and mingling with a whole variety of different people.

13 SUNDAY

Moon Age Day 1 Moon Sign Aquarius

am..

pm..

Today is about trying to keep your life as varied as possible, while refusing to be thrown by any sort of obstacles or problems. Once you have decided on a particular course of action, it would be sensible to stick to it, at least in the short term. A flexible approach is all very well, but it's not always possible.

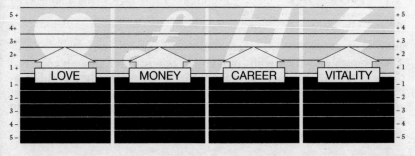

14 MONDAY   *Moon Age Day 2 Moon Sign Aquarius*

am ....

pm...

With the Moon in your solar twelfth house at the beginning of the week, you are encouraged to take life steadily. This offers you an ideal opportunity to ponder over any matters that have been on your mind for a while. Spending time in the company of people who mean a great deal to you also suits the current influences.

15 TUESDAY   *Moon Age Day 3 Moon Sign Pisces*

am ....

pm...

As the lunar high arrives, you have scope to tap into much more luck now than has been the case since the start of the year. You might decide to apply this to financial matters, but in most respects it is the social side of your life that should prosper. Getting on with people you haven't always seen eye to eye with is part of the scenario.

16 WEDNESDAY   *Moon Age Day 4 Moon Sign Pisces*

am ....

pm...

The Moon continues to reside in your zodiac sign, offering one of the most productive and potentially lucky periods of the month. Whatever you take on today, go for gold. It's time to let people know you are around, and show even those people who think they know you well that there is more to you than meets the eye.

17 THURSDAY   *Moon Age Day 5 Moon Sign Aries*

am ....

pm...

There's nothing wrong with confiding in others today, though you need to be prepared for disappointment. Not everyone might be either as reliable or as secretive as you would wish. It's natural to be suspicious but your intuition is to the fore, and if you listen to it you should know who to trust.

18 FRIDAY

Moon Age Day 6   Moon Sign Aries

am ....

pm ....

The emphasis today is on dealing with various demands that are being made of you. Intimate relationships could require some effort, and you may also feel you need to offer support to family members. Just remember that you would benefit from some time to yourself. Be prepared to consider your own requirements.

19 SATURDAY

Moon Age Day 7   Moon Sign Aries

am ....

pm ....

Trends now assist you to come back into the social mainstream. It's a good idea to plan what you want to do for the rest of the weekend, though you would be wise to remember that your energy levels are not unlimited. If you are going to seek some help with a particular task at work, make sure you listen to what is being said.

20 SUNDAY

Moon Age Day 8   Moon Sign Taurus

am ....

pm ....

Your ability to organise things is not particularly highlighted at the moment. The best way round this is to avoid getting yourself into situations that you know are going to be awkward and seek some wise advice from friends. If you do get yourself out of your depth, don't be afraid to ask people to lend a hand.

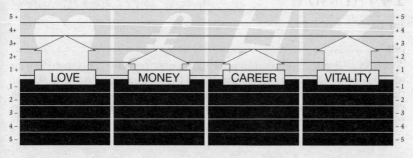

21 MONDAY
Moon Age Day 9 Moon Sign Taurus

am ....

pm...

Mixing with people who have the gift of the gab can be very appealing. However, you need to make sure you don't allow yourself to be duped by anyone simply because they spin a good yarn. This would not be an ideal day for making major decisions, particularly those that are made on impulse. Rational thought is required.

22 TUESDAY
Moon Age Day 10 Moon Sign Gemini

am ....

pm...

If you are going to get the best out of today, you need to be prepared to deal with any mishaps that occur. Rather than panicking, either start your task again at the beginning or seek the help and advice of someone who is an expert in their field. Capitalise on the opportunities that increased popularity offers.

23 WEDNESDAY
Moon Age Day 11 Moon Sign Gemini

am ....

pm...

Ask yourself whether you can really believe everything you hear. Even if there isn't anyone deliberately pulling the wool over your eyes, that's the way it might seem. Analyse situations carefully and only act when you know you have thought things through very carefully. If in doubt, rely on friends.

24 THURSDAY
Moon Age Day 12 Moon Sign Gemini

am ....

pm...

A period of significant financial potential is now on offer. This would be an ideal time to ensure that ideas you had in the past can now mature. Rather than worrying about situations you can't control, focus on feathering your own nest, as well as those of other people. This is about as selfish as Pisces gets, so make the most of it!

25 FRIDAY

Moon Age Day 13 Moon Sign Cancer

am ....

pm ....

There is always a dreamy side to the generally retiring sign of Pisces, and this is where the emphasis lies today. Conforming to expectations might not be easy, especially in a social sense. Even if part of you wants to retreat into your own little world, you still need to take into account the requirements of the day.

26 SATURDAY

Moon Age Day 14 Moon Sign Cancer

am ....

pm ....

Dealings with a slightly wider social circle give you a chance to come out of yourself more. Still, there could be a quiet sort of longing inside you for something you can't identify. This is the lot of Pisces, though you needn't allow the feeling to last too long. Try to keep yourself busy and be ready to seek new responsibilities at work.

27 SUNDAY

Moon Age Day 15 Moon Sign Leo

am ....

pm ....

It doesn't matter how much you rehearse, you can't always prepare for what lies ahead. Being in the public eye during the coming week could be one such instance. Don't let thoughts about this spoil your Sunday. Trends give you every assistance to cope with anything between now and next weekend.

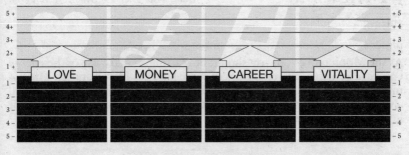

28 MONDAY *Moon Age Day 16 Moon Sign Leo*

am ....

pm ....

Even if you decide to put some of your ambitions on hold, that needn't prevent you from taking advantage of a fairly eventful start to the week. When it comes to looking at specific tasks, it's worth remembering that each passing day offers a chance to move closer to achieving a longed-for and important objective.

29 TUESDAY *Moon Age Day 17 Moon Sign Virgo*

am ....

pm ....

This is the second lunar low of the year. That is the time each month during which the Moon occupies your opposite sign of Virgo. It's an interlude that works best if you take things easy, perhaps by choosing to spend some time on your own. This is not the best day of the month for taking chances.

30 WEDNESDAY *Moon Age Day 18 Moon Sign Virgo*

am ....

pm ....

Despite the lunar low, you are in a good position to overcome reversals that have been around since late last year. This is particularly true at work, where you have what it takes to make a good impression on others. Remember that getting ahead of yourself with certain tasks should allow you to take time out to do something else.

31 THURSDAY *Moon Age Day 19 Moon Sign Virgo*

am ....

pm ....

As the Moon moves on, you should be starting to make use of the energy you have available, and an outing of some kind could well appeal. There is much to be said for spending time with family or friends, and you should also make the most of romantic contacts. If you have been looking for love, focus your attention now.

1 FRIDAY

Moon Age Day 20 Moon Sign Libra

am...

pm...

Today could well offer you plenty of opportunity to please yourself. Avoid getting too tied up with domestic issues, since at least some of these might sort themselves out if you give them time. Instead, why not do something that you find really interesting? Happiness is to be found with other people.

2 SATURDAY

Moon Age Day 21 Moon Sign Libra

am...

pm...

This would be an ideal time to resolve any outstanding issues in the professional arena. However, arguing isn't the best way to achieve this, and patience is definitely the order of the day. You have the confidence to do the right thing in the relationship stakes, and you need to be ready to show it now.

3 SUNDAY

Moon Age Day 22 Moon Sign Scorpio

am...

pm...

This may not be the most dynamic day of the month. Keep in mind that the Sun is in your solar twelfth house, which is a double-edged sword as far as you are concerned. It offers improved luck, but it also brings a more contemplative influence that does little to assist your forward progress. For this reason, take a considered view of life.

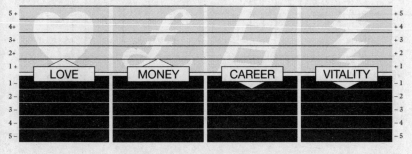

YOUR MONTH AT A GLANCE

$\bigoplus$ = Opportunities are around $\ominus$ = Be on the defensive $\bullet$ = Life is pretty ordinary

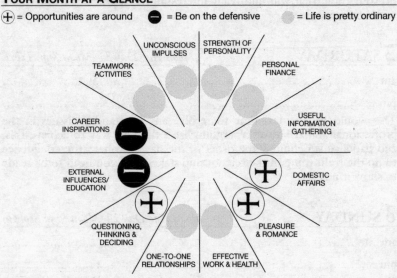

- UNCONSCIOUS IMPULSES
- STRENGTH OF PERSONALITY
- TEAMWORK ACTIVITIES
- PERSONAL FINANCE
- CAREER INSPIRATIONS
- USEFUL INFORMATION GATHERING
- EXTERNAL INFLUENCES/ EDUCATION
- DOMESTIC AFFAIRS
- QUESTIONING, THINKING & DECIDING
- PLEASURE & ROMANCE
- ONE-TO-ONE RELATIONSHIPS
- EFFECTIVE WORK & HEALTH

FEBRUARY HIGHS AND LOWS

Here I show you how the rhythms of the Moon will affect you this month. Like the tide, your energies and abilities will rise and fall with its pattern. When it is above the centre line, go for it, when it is below, you should be resting.

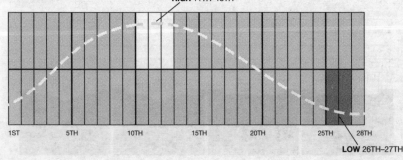

HIGH 11TH–13TH

1ST 5TH 10TH 15TH 20TH 25TH 28TH

LOW 26TH–27TH

4 MONDAY   *Moon Age Day 23 Moon Sign Scorpio*

am ....

pm ....

Your social life benefits from some positive trends so make the most of them! At the start of this working week there is less focus on working hard and more on having a good time. There are benefits to be gained now by putting at least some of your efforts into making headway in the popularity stakes.

5 TUESDAY   *Moon Age Day 24 Moon Sign Sagittarius*

am ....

pm ....

Try to avoid putting yourself under any undue pressure today. You have scope to achieve most of what you want, without having to push too hard. There is a continuing risk this month that you could spin off the track if you are not watching what you are doing as well as you might. Do your best to concentrate.

6 WEDNESDAY   *Moon Age Day 25 Moon Sign Sagittarius*

am ....

pm ....

Even if you find yourself in a position to manipulate others, that doesn't mean you have to do so. The Pisces nature is kind and sympathetic, and doesn't usually relish being a power broker. Although you can't expect to achieve everything you want, it is finding happiness that counts the most.

7 THURSDAY   *Moon Age Day 26 Moon Sign Capricorn*

am ....

pm ....

There is room in everyone's life for cultural improvements, and that includes Pisces. Anything that takes you out of yourself and which feeds your imagination is favoured now. However, that doesn't mean you have to settle for anything that is too low brow. Stick to your guns, even if some people have other ideas.

8 FRIDAY
Moon Age Day 27 Moon Sign Capricorn

am ....

pm...

Today will probably seem more satisfying with the benefit of hindsight, so there's no reason to worry if you can't get everything going your way. It pays to enlist the support and friendship of people you like, and to take steps to strengthen your popularity. You should have plenty of chances to do that at present.

9 SATURDAY
Moon Age Day 28 Moon Sign Aquarius

am ....

pm...

Despite your personal flair and undoubted confidence at the moment, you can't expect to have everything your own way. If this is down to people who are determined to throw a spanner in the works, there might be very little you can do about it. Keeping your eyes and ears open should help.

10 SUNDAY
Moon Age Day 0 Moon Sign Aquarius

am ....

pm...

Vitality could be somewhat low for the next couple of days, though if you are on a roll you might not notice the fact. The Moon is in your solar twelfth house, which is far from being bad in the case of Pisces. However, it does indicate a quieter interlude in which a more contemplative approach is called for.

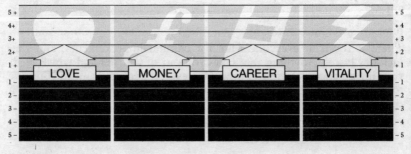

11 MONDAY
Moon Age Day 1 Moon Sign Pisces

am...

pm...

It ought to be possible for you to coast towards your chosen destination today. The lunar high offers more than a modicum of good luck for you to utilise, and in any case your technical skills are particularly emphasised at the moment. Rushing your fences isn't necessary right now in order for you to come out ahead.

12 TUESDAY
Moon Age Day 2 Moon Sign Pisces

am...

pm...

Today can be filled with promise, plus a good deal of excitement if you are in the market for it. Conforming to expectations might not be very easy at this time, but if you prove to others that you are good to know, they probably won't mind! On the contrary, it is your unorthodox way of doing things that is part of your appeal just now.

13 WEDNESDAY
Moon Age Day 3 Moon Sign Pisces

am...

pm...

You now have scope to achieve things that you have been working towards for quite some time. A mixture of patience and persistence is what really makes the difference, and you need to show that you possess these qualities. Few should deny you your moment of glory, and anyone who does is probably not worth considering.

14 THURSDAY
Moon Age Day 4 Moon Sign Aries

am...

pm...

Today is about your willingness to become the centre of attention. This might not be something you set out to do, though you need to be prepared for it all the same. Look for opportunities to get yourself into the good books of influential people, particularly at work. Advancement is on offer this month, though you have to believe in yourself.

15 FRIDAY

Moon Age Day 5 Moon Sign Aries

am ....

pm..

Recent small successes can now be turned into something more, though you will need to concentrate and you shouldn't allow others to make either the running or the decisions. Your mind is very astute at present, giving you a strong instinct for what is right in a given situation. This assists you to increase your level of confidence.

16 SATURDAY

Moon Age Day 6 Moon Sign Taurus

am ....

pm..

You should have a chance enjoy the cut and thrust of relationships this Saturday, and can gain a great deal simply from being around people who are successful in their own right. Trends now indicate a small but growing desire to break out of specific social or personal constraints, and it's up to you whether you act upon this.

17 SUNDAY

Moon Age Day 7 Moon Sign Taurus

am ....

pm..

There is a good deal of useful input available to you now, and it appears that you have all it takes to make ground over your competitors. You might think that would be difficult on a Sunday, but fate offers some significant opportunities. It is simply a matter of keeping your eyes open.

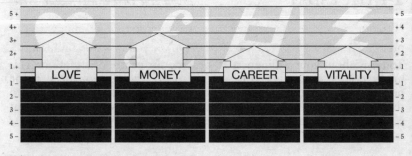

18 MONDAY
Moon Age Day 8 Moon Sign Gemini

am...

pm...

It might now be necessary for you to take a more dominant role in your family, and this has potential to be a very good thing. Does it feel to you as if you are lording it over others? You need to ensure that this is definitely not the case. Partnerships of all sorts are well highlighted under present planetary trends.

19 TUESDAY
Moon Age Day 9 Moon Sign Gemini

am...

pm...

The spotlight is now on your stamina, which assists you to achieve a good deal, simply by bulldozing your way through. This is very different from your usual sensitive approach, but it does allow you to make rapid progress in a number of different spheres. If your memory lets you down, perhaps you are overloading it.

20 WEDNESDAY
Moon Age Day 10 Moon Sign Gemini

am...

pm...

You might be tempted to hang back if you think that too much is being expected of you. This is an ideal time to talk things through with others, being honest and putting forward a rational point of view. It pays to show how confident you are when you are dealing with projects you understand.

21 THURSDAY
Moon Age Day 11 Moon Sign Cancer

am...

pm...

You can afford to keep up a higher profile today, and this should assist you to mix with some interesting types. There are career moves on offer for some Pisces people, though you might turn an offer down if you feel it isn't going in the direction you would wish. Keep an eye open for some quite amazing possibilities socially.

22 FRIDAY

Moon Age Day 12 Moon Sign Cancer

am ....

pm...

This would be a favourable time to think carefully about personal issues, and maybe even to seek to change the ground rules with regard to a specific relationship. Be prepared to welcome people you haven't seen for some time back into your life soon, and make the most of the news that they bring.

23 SATURDAY   ☿

Moon Age Day 13 Moon Sign Leo

am ....

pm...

It's natural to feel sometimes that specific jobs are more trouble than they are worth. That could well be the case this weekend, and the reason is simple. There is an emphasis now on having fun, and you won't take kindly to being held back. Decisive action is possible, even though you might wonder where it came from.

24 SUNDAY   ☿

Moon Age Day 14 Moon Sign Leo

am ....

pm...

Money-making endeavours are well starred and continue to be so between now and the middle of next week. Even if you don't want to take too many chances, you do have a sort of astrological guardian angel looking over you. When it comes to putting forward your unique point of view, simply tell it how it is!

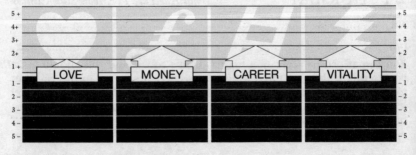

25 MONDAY ☿ *Moon Age Day 15 Moon Sign Leo*

am ....

pm ....

Be ready to capitalise on any opportunity to make new and influential business contacts. This is especially relevant if you are self-employed or in a management position. Outside work, this interlude can be very useful for pursuing social gatherings that you find fascinating. You needn't allow shyness to hold you back.

26 TUESDAY ☿ *Moon Age Day 16 Moon Sign Virgo*

am ....

pm ....

The lunar low is a chance to attend to unfinished business and get the decks cleared for action later on. Even if confidence isn't too easy to come by, you should still be able to get most things going your way. Given the limited luck on offer, there are good reasons to put any particularly ambitious plans on hold.

27 WEDNESDAY ☿ *Moon Age Day 17 Moon Sign Virgo*

am ....

pm ....

This is an ideal day to catch up with intimate relationships, and to spend some time in the bosom of your family. Nobody is forcing you down this road and in any case, this temporary respite can be extremely useful to you. It's a chance to focus on the planning and scheming that is taking place at the back of your mind.

28 THURSDAY ☿ *Moon Age Day 18 Moon Sign Libra*

am ....

pm ....

A period of favourable social highlights is now within your grasp. You have what it takes to streak out of the lunar low with all your positive qualities showing to the full. So many planetary trends are working well at the moment that there was never any reason for you to let the position of the Moon slow you down too much.

1 FRIDAY ☿ *Moon Age Day 19 Moon Sign Libra*

am ....

pm..

Be prepared to deal with obstacles when it comes to dealing with others. You can't expect everyone to behave as predicted, and your own attitude can also have a part to play. That famous Piscean patience can make all the difference on occasions today, though it might not be easy to find it!

2 SATURDAY ☿ *Moon Age Day 20 Moon Sign Scorpio*

am ....

pm..

Sociable trends are on the increase, assisting you to talk to just about anyone at present. Look out for invitations, and be ready to make the most of them, even if this means you have to put yourself in the spotlight in some way. There are signs that your receptiveness to romantic overtures may not be at its highest.

3 SUNDAY ☿ *Moon Age Day 21 Moon Sign Scorpio*

am ....

pm..

Finances can be strengthened today, and trends suggest that this may come through action you take now to consolidate a position you chose last week. You may also now be able to reap the benefits of decisions you took some weeks or months ago. It pays to recognise the needs that friends have of you at present, and to show them some special support if appropriate.

LOVE	MONEY	CAREER	VITALITY

March

2013

YOUR MONTH AT A GLANCE

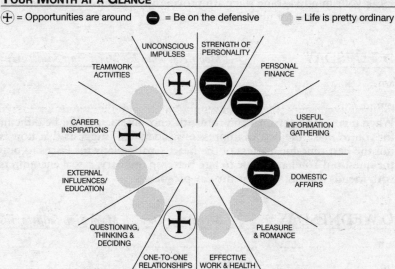

(+) = Opportunities are around ⬤ = Be on the defensive ⬤ = Life is pretty ordinary

UNCONSCIOUS IMPULSES (+)

STRENGTH OF PERSONALITY ⬤

TEAMWORK ACTIVITIES ⬤

PERSONAL FINANCE ⬤

CAREER INSPIRATIONS (+)

USEFUL INFORMATION GATHERING

EXTERNAL INFLUENCES/ EDUCATION

DOMESTIC AFFAIRS ⬤

QUESTIONING, THINKING & DECIDING

PLEASURE & ROMANCE

ONE-TO-ONE RELATIONSHIPS (+)

EFFECTIVE WORK & HEALTH

MARCH HIGHS AND LOWS

Here I show you how the rhythms of the Moon will affect you this month. Like the tide, your energies and abilities will rise and fall with its pattern. When it is above the centre line, go for it, when it is below, you should be resting.

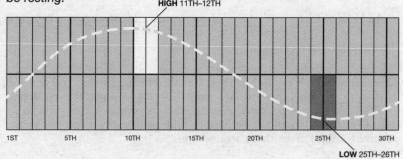

HIGH 11TH–12TH

1ST 5TH 10TH 15TH 20TH 25TH 30TH

LOW 25TH–26TH

4 MONDAY ☿ *Moon Age Day 22 Moon Sign Sagittarius*

am ....

pm ....

Trends encourage you to be especially sensitive to the feelings of those around you as this new week gets underway. Even if you want to please everyone, this may not be possible, particularly if you are determined to speak your mind at some stage. Improving your finances means holding on tight to money for now.

5 TUESDAY ☿ *Moon Age Day 23 Moon Sign Sagittarius*

am ....

pm ....

When it comes to personal and romantic encounters, it might be difficult for you to make the best of impressions today. This suggests that now is not the best time for matters of the heart – particularly for Pisces to pop the question! You have scope to fare better in ordinary, casual encounters with friends and associates as the day progresses.

6 WEDNESDAY ☿ *Moon Age Day 24 Moon Sign Sagittarius*

am ....

pm ....

This has potential to be another pleasurable period when it comes to getting a good deal of what you want from others. Your powers of communication are well accented at this time, and if you put them to good use, you shouldn't have to ask twice. You might even decide to turn a former adversary into a friend.

7 THURSDAY ☿ *Moon Age Day 25 Moon Sign Capricorn*

am ....

pm ....

There are signs that not only do you seek the limelight today, you demand it. If you can't get others to take notice of you, you might even decide to pull some sort of outrageous stunt, such is your determination to be seen. Confidence shouldn't be hard to find, particularly if you can attract positive feedback from those around you.

8 FRIDAY ☿ *Moon Age Day 26 Moon Sign Capricorn*

am ....

pm..

If certain social developments are under some stress now, one option is for you to choose to stay out of the public gaze. Spending time on your own is no real hardship, and there is happiness to be found in your own opinions and company. There is much to be said for learning how to do an old job in a new way.

9 SATURDAY ☿ *Moon Age Day 27 Moon Sign Aquarius*

am ....

pm..

It's important to take a realistic view of relationships at this time. Finding out exactly where you stand with specific individuals can help you to avoid embarrassment for all concerned, including yourself. Today could also offer a chance to look again at someone who has come to your attention recently.

10 SUNDAY ☿ *Moon Age Day 28 Moon Sign Aquarius*

am ....

pm..

What an excellent time this would be for getting new projects off the ground. The power of your personality is emphasised, and you have what it takes to turn heads in no uncertain terms. Be ready to use your charm on almost anyone, particularly if it helps you to get yourself into the right sort of company to advance.

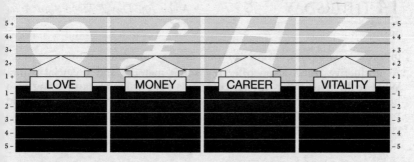

11 MONDAY ☿ *Moon Age Day 29 Moon Sign Pisces*

am ....

pm ....

The Moon returns to your zodiac sign, offering a crackerjack of a day, with plenty to set it apart and no lack of opportunity to gain attention. Now is the time to take a slight chance financially because good luck is there for the taking. Conforming to expectations might be hard, but you can get away with it now.

12 TUESDAY ☿ *Moon Age Day 0 Moon Sign Pisces*

am ....

pm ....

This would be as good a day as any to chance your arm. With the lunar high there to help you out, and everything to play for, the time is right to get cracking and show the world what you are made of. Don't be afraid to seek assistance and support from relatives and friends when you need it the most.

13 WEDNESDAY ☿ *Moon Age Day 1 Moon Sign Aries*

am ....

pm ....

It's possible that you have recently found it rather more difficult than usual to get through to loved ones. You are now in a position to change this situation. It's time to show how deep your sincerity actually runs, and to persuade them to explain how they view the situation. Reaching an understanding is what today is about.

14 THURSDAY ☿ *Moon Age Day 2 Moon Sign Aries*

am ....

pm ....

A productive trend is on offer regarding material and financial issues. What really makes the difference now is your willingness to bring to a head any matters that have been on your mind for some time. This could be useful for coming to terms with specific family members with whom you've had difficulty dealing lately.

15 FRIDAY ☿ *Moon Age Day 3 Moon Sign Taurus*

am...

pm...

A few of the negative elements of life surround personal attachments at the moment, which is why it's worth keeping things as light and casual as you can for today. Why not stick with friends, particularly those who don't make too many demands on you? Bringing new people into your life at this time can offer some interesting input.

16 SATURDAY ☿ *Moon Age Day 4 Moon Sign Taurus*

am...

pm...

It might be necessary to make some compromises today, and this fact won't be at all welcome in your life. Your best approach is to stop and think first, and see whether it's possible to get what you want and to please other people at the same time. Just remember, there is more than one way to skin any cat!

17 SUNDAY ☿ *Moon Age Day 5 Moon Sign Taurus*

am...

pm...

It's clear that you cannot please all of the people all of the time today and it might be something of a mistake to even try doing so. You would be wise to keep away from anyone who seems determined to throw a spanner in the social works. Concentrate instead on those individuals who have your own vested interest in a peaceful life.

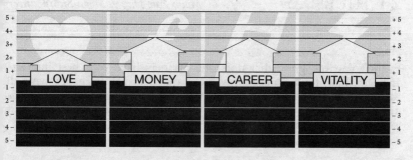

18 MONDAY ☿ *Moon Age Day 6 Moon Sign Gemini*

am ....

pm...

There should be plenty to keep you interested today, the only real problem being whether or not you have the time to fit in everything that takes your fancy. If a particular task or interest has been tiring you of late, perhaps you need to leave it alone. You can afford to give plenty of assistance to family members who need it now.

19 TUESDAY *Moon Age Day 7 Moon Sign Gemini*

am ....

pm...

Getting on with work and most practical jobs should be within your abilities today, even if you don't manage to make this the most progressive or successful day of the week. The situation won't be helped if you are constantly having to compensate for people who are unwilling or unable to do things correctly.

20 WEDNESDAY *Moon Age Day 8 Moon Sign Cancer*

am ....

pm...

You now have the ability to elicit some extremely promising responses from others, making this an excellent day for putting forward suggestions. There are several areas of your life that might work better with a little reorganisation. Now you have the chance to look at specifics and to deal with them.

21 THURSDAY *Moon Age Day 9 Moon Sign Cancer*

am ....

pm...

Even if you recognise that domestic partners have your best interests at heart, that doesn't necessarily mean that you will be happy with all their actions. It's worth considering whether your own mood is having a negative effect on your relationships with others just now. Be prepared to isolate yourself if this will help.

22 FRIDAY
Moon Age Day 10 Moon Sign Cancer

am...

pm...

The ability to attract the good things in life is particularly well accented now, so make hay while the sun shines! Personally speaking you have plenty going for you and can use the current influences to attract all sorts of attention, some of it quite unexpected. Your consideration for those around you is noteworthy.

23 SATURDAY
Moon Age Day 11 Moon Sign Leo

am...

pm...

In an organisational sense it should now be possible for you to get things going your way. Your sound judgement is enhanced by both your ability to grasp new concepts and your willingness to look ahead. Even in the face of doubts from those close to you, you can afford to keep ploughing onward.

24 SUNDAY
Moon Age Day 12 Moon Sign Leo

am...

pm...

Trends now indicate slow material progress and a feeling of being under pressure. These facts need not prevent you from forging ahead, even against quite difficult odds. It's time to show the brave side of your nature, and to ensure you give a good account of yourself in any dealings with others.

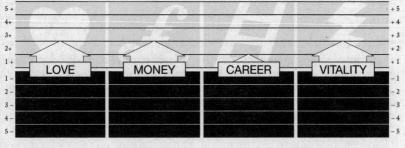

25 MONDAY
Moon Age Day 13 Moon Sign Virgo

am ....

pm ....

It could seem as though everyone is getting ahead faster than you are, and to a certain extent this may be true, for today at least. However, the lunar low doesn't last very long and you can manage to curb your enthusiasm for just a short time. There is much to be gained from conversations in the evening.

26 TUESDAY
Moon Age Day 14 Moon Sign Virgo

am ....

pm ....

The lunar low should not prove particularly potent this month, mainly because you can tap into some strong planetary support from other directions. Despite this, it would still be worth considering modifying some of your plans for the forthcoming days, as today may carry a few minor setbacks, though nothing you can't handle.

27 WEDNESDAY
Moon Age Day 15 Moon Sign Libra

am ....

pm ....

There are possible gains to be made in your love life, particularly if you are willing to communicate and allow your partner into the deepest recesses of that Piscean mind. In a business sense, new options could be available at any time now, assisting you to move closer to achieving some longed-for objectives.

28 THURSDAY
Moon Age Day 16 Moon Sign Libra

am ....

pm ....

What shows most pointedly right now is your natural curiosity. Anything and everything can capture your fertile imagination, and there is nothing that you consider too small to escape your 'need to know'. That's all very well, but it's important to make sure others don't think you are being nosy – even if you are!

29 FRIDAY
Moon Age Day 17 Moon Sign Libra

am...

pm...

You have what it takes to be fast and efficient in all practical matters today, and should be leaving others in no doubt whatsoever that you know what you are doing. In work situations, you have scope to do your own thing, so the expectations of others will hold little interest for you, no matter how nicely they are expressed.

30 SATURDAY
Moon Age Day 18 Moon Sign Scorpio

am...

pm...

The less pressure you put yourself under today, the more progress you should be able to make. Even if you've had trouble finding inspiration recently, you can now afford to be in a much more positive frame of mind. All the same, it pays to stick to what really interests you and leave worries on the back burner until Monday.

31 SUNDAY
Moon Age Day 19 Moon Sign Scorpio

am...

pm...

There are plenty of planetary influences about now that could help you to find exciting social encounters. You are in a position to seek out interesting and influential individuals, in terms of both work and your social life. Be prepared to deal with any disagreements between yourself and those you know very well.

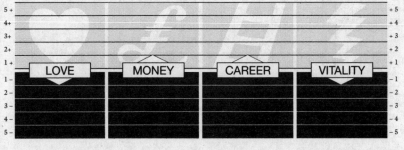

April

2013

YOUR MONTH AT A GLANCE

⊕ = Opportunities are around   ⊖ = Be on the defensive   ● = Life is pretty ordinary

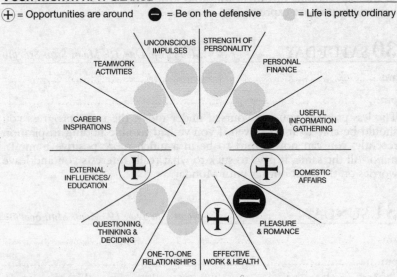

- STRENGTH OF PERSONALITY
- UNCONSCIOUS IMPULSES
- TEAMWORK ACTIVITIES
- PERSONAL FINANCE
- CAREER INSPIRATIONS
- USEFUL INFORMATION GATHERING
- EXTERNAL INFLUENCES/ EDUCATION
- DOMESTIC AFFAIRS
- QUESTIONING, THINKING & DECIDING
- PLEASURE & ROMANCE
- ONE-TO-ONE RELATIONSHIPS
- EFFECTIVE WORK & HEALTH

APRIL HIGHS AND LOWS

Here I show you how the rhythms of the Moon will affect you this month. Like the tide, your energies and abilities will rise and fall with its pattern. When it is above the centre line, go for it, when it is below, you should be resting.

HIGH 7TH–8TH

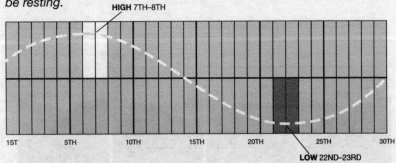

| 1ST | 5TH | 10TH | 15TH | 20TH | 25TH | 30TH |

LOW 22ND–23RD

1 MONDAY
Moon Age Day 20 Moon Sign Sagittarius

am..

pm..

Trends encourage you to put pleasure on your agenda as a new week commences. Although you are quite capable of working hard at this time, you should also be willing to take time out to simply enjoy yourself. On the way, you have an opportunity to bring joy to those around you, especially family members.

2 TUESDAY
Moon Age Day 21 Moon Sign Sagittarius

am..

pm..

Domestic circumstances are so well accented at present that you might not want to be anywhere but at home. Before taking offence at criticism you receive, you need to recognise that most people are actually on your side now. Be willing to seek compliments in both expected and unexpected directions.

3 WEDNESDAY
Moon Age Day 22 Moon Sign Capricorn

am..

pm..

You have everything you need today to get most matters proceeding pretty much as expected. However, you shouldn't be too quick to judge others, either by their actions or through what they are saying. Jumping to conclusions could lead you into hot water, particularly if you insist on indulging in gossip.

4 THURSDAY
Moon Age Day 23 Moon Sign Capricorn

am..

pm..

It's time to look out for monetary fluctuations and make the most of them to gain financially. You can be very astute at present, and should have no reason to falter over important decisions. Even if the whole world and his dog want to give you advice at this time, in the end it's your own opinions that count.

5 FRIDAY
Moon Age Day 24 Moon Sign Aquarius

am...

pm...

Now you are in a good position to bring important matters to a head. Don't be surprised if others try to interfere in your life, particularly on a personal level. Although your zodiac sign doesn't go looking for confrontation, it might be time to show specific individuals that you are no pushover.

6 SATURDAY
Moon Age Day 25 Moon Sign Aquarius

am...

pm...

Pisces can be the life and soul of the party this weekend, and it's up to you to make the most of this trend. There are also signs that you could find certain situations just a little trying, especially those in which you are expected to take on additional responsibilities or organise something that puts you firmly in the public eye.

7 SUNDAY
Moon Age Day 26 Moon Sign Pisces

am...

pm...

You may have been hovering on the brink of significant progress for a few days now. The lunar high offers the extra incentive to take life in your own hands and make it produce what you want. If that means being somewhat more selfish than usual, at least make sure you don't completely ignore the needs of others.

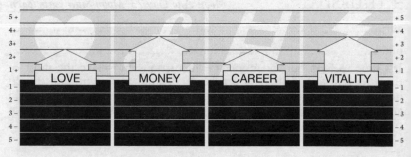

8 MONDAY
Moon Age Day 27 Moon Sign Pisces

am ....

pm...

Your persuasive powers are to the fore, and if there is something you particularly want to do, there's no reason to hold back. You have what it takes to persuade most people to follow your lead at the moment, even if you are making up your mind as you go along. It's time to show the sheer magnetism of your personality.

9 TUESDAY
Moon Age Day 28 Moon Sign Aries

am ....

pm...

This has potential to be one of the best days of the month socially speaking. The present position of Venus assists popularity, which you can use to your own advantage, as well as on behalf of others. Life is always a balance, and success today is simply a question of knowing how to tip the scales in your favour.

10 WEDNESDAY
Moon Age Day 0 Moon Sign Aries

am ....

pm...

There could well be plenty of demands coming your way at present, but that shouldn't matter if you are determined to let your confidence show. You would be wise to control the urge to spend too freely now. That way, you can be ready for any genuine bargains you identify in the very near future.

11 THURSDAY
Moon Age Day 1 Moon Sign Aries

am ....

pm...

If you find yourself under any sort of pressure to make changes to your personal life, you can afford to resist them for all you are worth. In the end only you can make up your mind about what you want, and the advice that comes from others may not be sound. If all else fails, use your powerful intuition to lead the way.

12 FRIDAY
Moon Age Day 2 Moon Sign Taurus

am ....

pm ....

A little speculation could well lead to accumulation at the moment. It's time to capitalise on the luck that is available, and to make sure your intuition plays a part in the scenario. Confidences from friends need to be guarded carefully, particularly since a few of your own secrets might surface at some stage right now.

13 SATURDAY
Moon Age Day 3 Moon Sign Taurus

am ....

pm ....

You now have everything you need to become the centre of attention. You are more settled within yourself than was the case previously, and this should help you to identify what you want from life. Take some time out to watch the flowers grow now that the spring has really arrived. A break can work wonders.

14 SUNDAY
Moon Age Day 4 Moon Sign Gemini

am ....

pm ....

A distinctly nostalgic phase is indicated at present, and might encourage you down memory lane in a big way. Even if there are warm and comforting aspects to your past, it is the future that really matters. It's not worth getting hung up on things that are long gone, especially when concentrating now can lead to positive results.

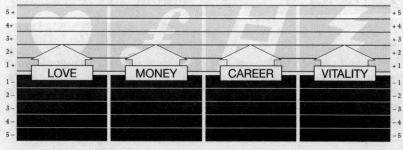

15 MONDAY
Moon Age Day 5 Moon Sign Gemini

am ....

pm ....

Sorting out the wheat from the chaff is important when it comes to getting on well, especially at work. Life can seem like a jigsaw puzzle at times, and under present influences it might be difficult for you to find all the pieces you need. Once again you have scope to obtain some timely advice and support from people around you.

16 TUESDAY
Moon Age Day 6 Moon Sign Gemini

am ....

pm ....

In your daily life you may be able to pursue some pleasant encounters, and enjoy some time to have fun. There's no reason to take anything too seriously this week, particularly if you can persuade those around you to join in. Get out and about if you can, because some sort of journey would suit the current astrological scene.

17 WEDNESDAY
Moon Age Day 7 Moon Sign Cancer

am ....

pm ....

Personal freedom is the key to contentment for Pisces at this time. Be prepared to insist on doing things your own way and to push extremely hard against any sort of opposition. Confidence shouldn't be lacking, even if you continue to approach matters in the quiet Pisces way.

18 THURSDAY
Moon Age Day 8 Moon Sign Cancer

am ....

pm ....

This is a period during which intimate and private matters can be a source of emotional fulfilment, which is always an important factor in the life of Pisces people. Are there any specific reasons to celebrate as a result of happenings within the family? If so, make sure you are the first one to put out the flags.

19 FRIDAY

Moon Age Day 9 Moon Sign Leo

am ....

pm...

Trends indicate a pronounced tendency towards criticism today. This is a quality that certainly has a part to play when you are faced with important decisions. The fact that you do not go blindly into any situation means you are simply being discriminating. This is especially important in terms of financial commitments at the present time.

20 SATURDAY

Moon Age Day 10 Moon Sign Leo

am ....

pm...

You can easily achieve any reasonable objectives you set yourself today, though you could also decide to retreat into yourself if you feel threatened in any way. By far the best response to any slight difficulties would be to face them squarely, though this course of action might not be as easy as it sounds for the moment.

21 SUNDAY

Moon Age Day 11 Moon Sign Leo

am ....

pm...

Be prepared to respond to unexpected happenings in your normal routine. If you remain flexible from the start, you needn't allow such eventualities to cause too much in the way of concern. All the same, keeping everything running smoothly might not be easy, and there is much to be said for seeking a little help from outside.

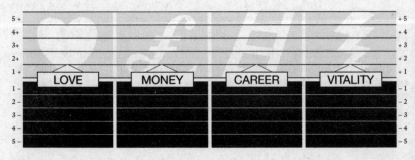

22 MONDAY
Moon Age Day 12 Moon Sign Virgo

am...

pm...

Playing it safe is the order of the day in professional matters, and keep in mind that it would be sensible to defer to the wisdom of people who know more about certain facts than you do. Allowing your limitations to occupy your thinking isn't wise though, because you risk losing some of the confidence you have in yourself at the moment.

23 TUESDAY
Moon Age Day 13 Moon Sign Virgo

am...

pm...

Though optimism and positive thinking go a long way at present, they might not be enough in themselves to ensure success. What you also need is application, which might be difficult during the continuing lunar low. The more sociable side to your nature is highlighted, and the desire to have fun is strong.

24 WEDNESDAY
Moon Age Day 14 Moon Sign Libra

am...

pm...

Your practical skills are well emphasised at this time. There's nothing wrong with undertaking jobs around the house yourself, even if you have never tackled them before. With increasing belief in your ability and the positive support you can elicit from your partner or family members, now is the time to get stuck in.

25 THURSDAY
Moon Age Day 15 Moon Sign Libra

am...

pm...

The Sun, now in your solar third house, brings a chance to capitalise on comings and goings. You ought to be able to make this a rather enjoyable time, particularly if you can keep your mind occupied. Coming up with ideas that are both original and of interest to others can certainly help you boost your popularity.

26 FRIDAY
Moon Age Day 16 Moon Sign Scorpio

am ....

pm..

Today can be especially progressive on the financial front, even if you are not actually doing anything specific. A greater understanding of your future options might show you that you have potential to end up better off than you thought. You certainly have not been too optimistic, a fact that you need to realise now.

27 SATURDAY
Moon Age Day 17 Moon Sign Scorpio

am ....

pm..

What matters for today is your versatility, and your willingness to offer the sort of help and advice to others that it seems only you can provide. The weekend can be good from a financial point of view, particularly if this turns out to be as a result of actions you took some time ago which are only now bearing fruit.

28 SUNDAY
Moon Age Day 18 Moon Sign Sagittarius

am ....

pm..

Be prepared to deal with some strong emotions today, even if most of them are being exhibited by other people. Everyone has a right to their own unique point of view, though this might not be convenient, and could lead to some disagreements. As usual, you have everything you need to play the honest broker.

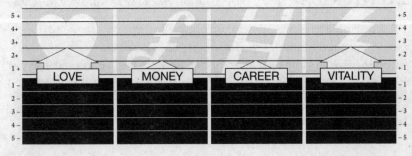

29 MONDAY   *Moon Age Day 19 Moon Sign Sagittarius*

am..

pm..

Trends encourage you to get down to business and look very carefully at the practical side of life. It's time to put your thinking head on and tackle problems, even those that are stumping others. Romance could be coming along under current influences, though it remains to be seen whether you have time to notice this fact.

30 TUESDAY   *Moon Age Day 20 Moon Sign Capricorn*

am..

pm..

Personal and intimate subject matter allows you to show your best side today. There are good reasons to seek support from loved ones and from special friends in whom you put a high degree of trust. Committing yourself to new projects might not be very easy just now. Why not defer any decisions until tomorrow?

1 WEDNESDAY   *Moon Age Day 21 Moon Sign Capricorn*

am..

pm..

You have what it takes to achieve the best of both worlds now. The domestic area of your life offers fulfilment, but significant progress is also possible at work. If you have the chance to embark on a journey soon, maybe even a long one, you have the means at your disposal to broaden your horizons.

2 THURSDAY   *Moon Age Day 22 Moon Sign Aquarius*

am..

pm..

Social and co-operative matters are positively highlighted, and much of the joy you can experience today comes through what you do on behalf of others. This is fairly typical of the sign of Pisces and can help you to make this a fulfilling period, during which you ought to feel a sense of rightness and balance.

3 FRIDAY

Moon Age Day 23 Moon Sign Aquarius

am ....

pm..

Minor pressures are possible, maybe relating to demands made of you by family members. This could be a little disappointing, particularly if you have been devoting plenty of attention to the domestic scene of late. All the same, a generally cheerful approach works best now, and assists you to take matters in your stride.

4 SATURDAY

Moon Age Day 24 Moon Sign Pisces

am ....

pm...

The lunar high should give you plenty of support today to push your ideas forward. The tendency to retreat into your own little world now disappears and you have scope to put yourself in the social flow and take your place in the world. Be ready to take advantage of all the luck that is available.

5 SUNDAY

Moon Age Day 25 Moon Sign Pisces

am ....

pm...

This could be the best time of the month to chance your arm. A cautious approach when it comes to cash would be no bad thing, though the auspices are very good right now. In addition, you need to show that you know how to have fun, and there is a very good chance that things fall in line as you would wish.

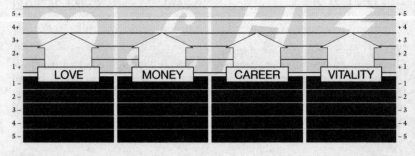

May

2013

YOUR MONTH AT A GLANCE

$\oplus$ = Opportunities are around   ⊖ = Be on the defensive   ⬤ = Life is pretty ordinary

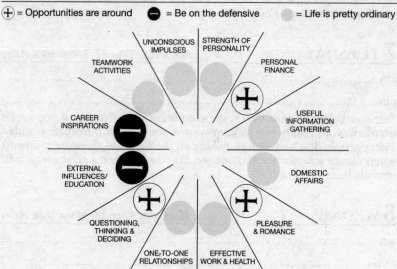

UNCONSCIOUS
IMPULSES

STRENGTH OF
PERSONALITY

TEAMWORK
ACTIVITIES

PERSONAL
FINANCE

CAREER
INSPIRATIONS

USEFUL
INFORMATION
GATHERING

EXTERNAL
INFLUENCES/
EDUCATION

DOMESTIC
AFFAIRS

QUESTIONING,
THINKING &
DECIDING

PLEASURE
& ROMANCE

ONE-TO-ONE
RELATIONSHIPS

EFFECTIVE
WORK & HEALTH

MAY HIGHS AND LOWS

Here I show you how the rhythms of the Moon will affect you this month. Like the tide, your energies and abilities will rise and fall with its pattern. When it is above the centre line, go for it, when it is below, you should be resting.

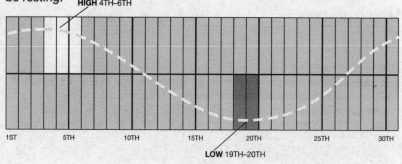

HIGH 4TH–6TH

1ST   5TH   10TH   15TH   20TH   25TH   30TH

LOW 19TH–20TH

81

6 MONDAY   *Moon Age Day 26 Moon Sign Pisces*

am ....

pm..

There is a solution to every problem, even ones that have been dogging you for quite some time. Once you have looked at matters carefully you should be able to address most issues. Good luck is generally still within your grasp, and it can be especially useful if you have to deal with situations that others find tricky.

7 TUESDAY   *Moon Age Day 27 Moon Sign Aries*

am ....

pm..

A few setbacks are possible on the communication front, and you might decide it would be better to keep your mouth closed on occasion today. Pisces people don't have to be talking all the time and there are moments when silence serves a better objective. You can still find a place for normal friendly banter, though.

8 WEDNESDAY   *Moon Age Day 28 Moon Sign Aries*

am ....

pm..

This is a period during which you can afford to let go of certain responsibilities and enjoy yourself. It's natural to feel that you haven't done everything you should have done by now, but you need to ask whether waiting a little while longer will really do any harm. Why not get out of the house and see something new?

9 THURSDAY   *Moon Age Day 29 Moon Sign Taurus*

am ....

pm..

Persuading others to show their most generous side can work wonders, and you need to take advantage of this fact. If people are willing to do you favours, it might be seen as churlish to refuse. Some care is necessary with money at the moment, particularly when it comes to impulse purchases.

10 FRIDAY

Moon Age Day 0 Moon Sign Taurus

am ....

pm..

A slight sense of urgency is indicated regarding emotional matters, though getting into deep discussions may not be your best option at this time. Keeping it light and easy is the ideal way of dealing with relationships today. Bear in mind that quite a few issues will look very different by the time tomorrow comes along.

11 SATURDAY

Moon Age Day 1 Moon Sign Gemini

am ....

pm..

There is no need for you to abandon personal freedoms at this time. On the contrary, you might even be more inclined to stick up for your rights today than would be the case on most occasions. Be careful that you don't tread on the toes of other people. Casual friendships have much to offer, including the opportunity for some amusing diversions.

12 SUNDAY

Moon Age Day 2 Moon Sign Gemini

am ....

pm..

In most social situations your easy-going and friendly attitude should assist you to attract a positive response from others. This can make for a very happy Sunday, with no lack of people to talk to and plenty going on that could even be termed exciting. Actually getting down to doing anything practical might not be so easy!

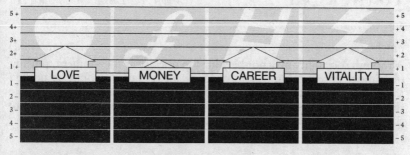

13 MONDAY
Moon Age Day 3 Moon Sign Gemini

am ....

pm ....

Even if you've managed to get a great deal that is of interest going on in your life as a whole, you might find some aspects distinctly tedious. The answer is quite simple. Concentrate on what brings you pleasure and leave other matters alone, at least for today. Pisces should be showing real creative flair at present.

14 TUESDAY
Moon Age Day 4 Moon Sign Cancer

am ....

pm ....

Once again it pays to demonstrate your willingness to see another attitude, or even belief pattern, that is very different to your own. You can't necessarily expect others to react in the same way, so your tolerance might well have to go that little bit further, particularly with much older or younger people.

15 WEDNESDAY
Moon Age Day 5 Moon Sign Cancer

am ....

pm ....

There are signs that specific arrangements may have to be altered at the last minute. You need to be ready to deal with disruptions, and with any resulting frustration. Ask yourself whether it would be worth holding back some of your plans for the moment. Patience should assist you to win through.

16 THURSDAY
Moon Age Day 6 Moon Sign Leo

am ....

pm ....

Although sociability may not be your top priority at the moment, putting on a more entertaining face in order to please others would be no bad thing. It's so much second nature to Pisces to serve humanity as a whole that it might feel as though you have little choice. The positive aspect of this is that it can help you to feel better yourself.

17 FRIDAY
Moon Age Day 7 Moon Sign Leo

am ....

pm ....

There are good reasons to take a favourable view of home and family today, and to make the most of the sociable side of your nature. This is an ideal time to look for love, and some of you may find it without looking at all! Casual conversations can help you to reach some quite sensational conclusions.

18 SATURDAY
Moon Age Day 8 Moon Sign Leo

am ....

pm ....

It pays to get as much variety into your life as you can. It is very important to do different things and not to take the usual route to any particular destination, physically or mentally. A holiday taken around this time would offer Pisces the best of all worlds, but if this isn't possible, it's up to you to find alternatives.

19 SUNDAY
Moon Age Day 9 Moon Sign Virgo

am ....

pm ....

Getting your own way in a monetary sense could prove very significant at the moment. These developments may be helped if you can turn on the charm and put forward a good, reasoned case. A degree of frugality may be necessary in the short term, if only to prove that you can live practically on fresh air. The lunar low should assist you in this.

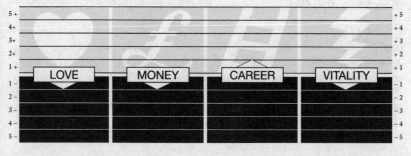

20 MONDAY
Moon Age Day 10 Moon Sign Virgo

am ....

pm..

You would be wise to be on your guard for the odd setback as the lunar low continues. You can't expect all your efforts to yield the results you wish, but that should prompt you to work harder than ever to make progress. However, there is nothing at all to prevent you from having a rest as well.

21 TUESDAY
Moon Age Day 11 Moon Sign Libra

am ....

pm..

The things you hear others saying can be of tremendous use to you today, so keep your ears open. You may find that if you take on board the ideas of people around you, you can build new enterprises of your own. Even if you can't get on well with everyone at the moment, important people should be a synch.

22 WEDNESDAY
Moon Age Day 12 Moon Sign Libra

am ....

pm..

Avoid overreaching yourself in terms of your ego. Whenever you go overboard and really begin to show tremendous confidence in yourself, there's a risk that something will happen to bring you down to earth. Showing a degree of that Pisces humility right from the start can make all the difference.

23 THURSDAY
Moon Age Day 13 Moon Sign Scorpio

am ....

pm..

Trends encourage you to turn your attention towards home once more, and to make the most of what others are doing to improve your comfort. Although this might take the wind out of your sails somewhat, you should take full advantage of the attention and genuine affection you can attract at the moment.

24 FRIDAY

Moon Age Day 14 Moon Sign Scorpio

am ....

pm...

Your love life has potential to be the most exciting and progressive area of life at the moment, particularly if you find forward movement in a general sense harder to achieve. The planet Venus occupies a favourable position, and you needn't be fazed by the fact that you are clinging tenaciously to existing attachments.

25 SATURDAY

Moon Age Day 15 Moon Sign Sagittarius

am ....

pm...

Once again issues of love and romance can offer plenty of rewards now. You also have more room for self-expression in social issues, and there is much to be said for standing out in any crowd. The implications for the weekend are positive, and present trends offer opportunities for a happy time.

26 SUNDAY

Moon Age Day 16 Moon Sign Sagittarius

am ....

pm...

The spotlight is now on domestic harmony. Once again Venus makes its presence felt, assisting you to create a happy time around your home. You have what it takes to deal with family members, and it is possible you won't feel the need to go any further than your own living room to be truly contented.

5 +				+ 5
4+				+ 4
3+				+ 3
2+				+ 2
1 +				+ 1
LOVE	MONEY	CAREER	VITALITY	
1 -				- 1
2 -				- 2
3 -				- 3
4 -				- 4
5 -				- 5

27 MONDAY
Moon Age Day 17 Moon Sign Capricorn

am ....

pm ....

There are only so many things you can control at once, so if you are tiring with the strain of it all, why not delegate some of the responsibility? It's worth identifying people around you who can be persuaded to lend a hand. Meanwhile, you have a chance to find new ways to fill your leisure hours.

28 TUESDAY
Moon Age Day 18 Moon Sign Capricorn

am ....

pm ....

Looking and feeling at your best today is what the current interlude is all about. Socially and romantically, you need to find situations that seem tailor-made to suit your requirements. Today works best if you keep confrontations to a minimum and make romance number one on your agenda.

29 WEDNESDAY
Moon Age Day 19 Moon Sign Aquarius

am ....

pm ....

Be ready to get the very best from family members and people you care for generally. This is relevant whether or not you are spending a great deal of time at home. Bear in mind that some of the pressures you feel at the moment could be related to being in the limelight, a place where you are unlikely to feel at ease.

30 THURSDAY
Moon Age Day 20 Moon Sign Aquarius

am ....

pm ....

Quick thinking comes in handy today, and you shouldn't have any difficulty functioning at full strength. However, you might also be focusing your mind on places you care for deeply and which you might not have seen for a while. You can afford to feel generally comfortable with personal and romantic attachments.

31 FRIDAY
Moon Age Day 21 Moon Sign Aquarius

am...

pm...

There is much to be said for making a splash, though that might not be as easy as it sounds. Take heart, because tomorrow the lunar high arrives and brings with it a whole new series of incentives. For the moment, it's worth spending what time you can with good friends, encouraging and being encouraged.

1 SATURDAY
Moon Age Day 22 Moon Sign Pisces

am...

pm...

This is a favourable period in which to work on new plans and schemes. There is support to be gained around every corner, some of it coming from directions you might never have expected. Even if the going gets tough today, you need to show that you are equal to any reasonable challenge you set yourself.

2 SUNDAY
Moon Age Day 23 Moon Sign Pisces

am...

pm...

Today is all about communication and what you can gain from this two-way process. Your level of decisiveness and confidence may not be exactly what you would wish, but this won't matter if you realise how much support you can attract. An ideal time to make specific changes to your working arrangements.

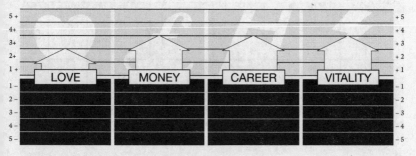

June

2013

YOUR MONTH AT A GLANCE

$\oplus$ = Opportunities are around $\ominus$ = Be on the defensive $\bigcirc$ = Life is pretty ordinary

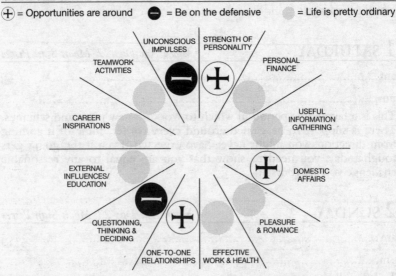

UNCONSCIOUS IMPULSES

STRENGTH OF PERSONALITY

TEAMWORK ACTIVITIES

PERSONAL FINANCE

CAREER INSPIRATIONS

USEFUL INFORMATION GATHERING

EXTERNAL INFLUENCES/ EDUCATION

DOMESTIC AFFAIRS

QUESTIONING, THINKING & DECIDING

PLEASURE & ROMANCE

ONE-TO-ONE RELATIONSHIPS

EFFECTIVE WORK & HEALTH

JUNE HIGHS AND LOWS

Here I show you how the rhythms of the Moon will affect you this month. Like the tide, your energies and abilities will rise and fall with its pattern. When it is above the centre line, go for it, when it is below, you should be resting. **HIGH** 1ST–2ND

HIGH 28TH–29TH

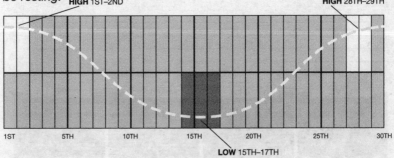

| 1ST | 5TH | 10TH | 15TH | 20TH | 25TH | 30TH |

LOW 15TH–17TH

90

3 MONDAY
Moon Age Day 24 Moon Sign Aries

am ....

pm ....

A talkative approach is the order of the day today, and your active mind and quick tongue might leave others trailing behind. Even if you are experiencing many extremes right now, you should be able to cope. Be ready to deal with minor arguments in family situations. Hold your ground – this is no time to be fazed!

4 TUESDAY
Moon Age Day 25 Moon Sign Aries

am ....

pm ....

The emphasis today is on actively seeking to broaden your horizons in just about any way you can manage. Those Pisces people who have chosen to take a holiday around now are probably the luckiest, but there are gains to be made, even if you can't get away from the usual routines.

5 WEDNESDAY
Moon Age Day 26 Moon Sign Taurus

am ....

pm ....

It's tempting to allow the past to loom large in your consideration of the present. Even if it's somewhat difficult to shake yourself free of this at the moment, there are good reasons to try. It's time to commit yourself to new strategies and let go of issues that can have no possible part to play in your thinking now.

6 THURSDAY
Moon Age Day 27 Moon Sign Taurus

am ....

pm ....

Modest progress at work is indicated, though that shouldn't prevent you from thinking about greater gain and more rapid advancement. Why not persuade colleagues to help, particularly those who have shown themselves to be trustworthy. Meanwhile, younger individuals have a great deal to offer you at home.

7 FRIDAY
Moon Age Day 28 Moon Sign Taurus

am ....

pm...

It pays to find some quality time that you can spend with loved ones. You can afford to offer plenty of help to those you care about the most, both at this time and over the next few days. Rather than seeing the effort you have to put in for them as a chore, why not view it as a privilege?

8 SATURDAY
Moon Age Day 0 Moon Sign Gemini

am ....

pm...

There is much to be said for pursuing rewards in the domestic sphere at the moment, though it could be practical and professional matters that offer you scope to achieve the greatest level of advancement. If you can persuade other people to listen to what you have to say, your progress now can be impressive indeed.

9 SUNDAY
Moon Age Day 1 Moon Sign Gemini

am ....

pm...

There are signs that getting through to younger people might not be easy at the moment, but it is worth the effort. Be ready to deal with little troubles early on, but by the middle of the day you should be making rapid progress again, especially in the direction of change. A strong desire to travel is now indicated.

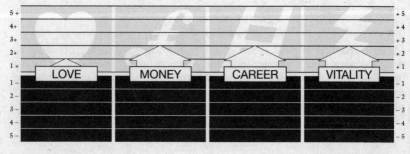

10 MONDAY
Moon Age Day 2 Moon Sign Cancer

am..

pm..

This would not be a good day to bottle up your emotions, and in any case, under prevailing planetary conditions it probably isn't necessary. Your best approach is simply to speak your mind, even if to do so seems in some way difficult. Once you have spilled the beans, you are in a position to move on.

11 TUESDAY
Moon Age Day 3 Moon Sign Cancer

am..

pm..

Irritations are a distinct possibility, especially at work. Responding to these means turning the pressure up and making certain you get your own way. Right now you have the power to make certain demands. It's possible that some people will be so surprised that they will follow your lead without thinking or arguing.

12 WEDNESDAY
Moon Age Day 4 Moon Sign Cancer

am..

pm..

All you have to do to make the most of today is to let your light shine more brightly. You have everything you need to attract innumerable compliments from the people around you, though of course they mean nothing if you won't accept them. Spend at least part of today concentrating on having a good time.

13 THURSDAY
Moon Age Day 5 Moon Sign Leo

am..

pm..

Your sense of optimism and your thirst for new ideas are what you should be showing to the world at present. There is also a focus on your health and well-being, and on the efforts you are making to improve them. Why not plan ahead and make something special of the forthcoming weekend?

14 FRIDAY

Moon Age Day 6 Moon Sign Leo

am ....

pm...

If domestic or family matters appear to be too confining today, this could increase your desire to get away, maybe into the country or, better still for you, to the coast. Opting to take a trip can make a real difference now, the more so if you choose to take a favoured pal or your partner with you.

15 SATURDAY

Moon Age Day 7 Moon Sign Virgo

am ....

pm...

Unexpected delays are possible, and in addition, it might be difficult to persuade other people to be fully supportive. You can deal with all of this and still come out smiling. The fact is that once you have the bit between your teeth, it will take more than an adverse position of the Moon to hold you back.

16 SUNDAY

Moon Age Day 8 Moon Sign Virgo

am ....

pm...

If instant success isn't an option today, you will simply have to settle for a steady sort of progress. Even if the lunar low doesn't have as strong a negative bearing on your life this month as is sometimes the case, it does encourage a slower interlude. However, this could give you an opportunity to examine your finances in some detail.

17 MONDAY   *Moon Age Day 9 Moon Sign Virgo*

am ....

pm..

It's vital now that you take a realistic view of what you can obtain from other people. If you don't, you could be in for the odd disappointment. Be aware of any reasons for congratulations in your domestic circle, and make sure you aren't the last to offer them. All in all, this works best as a family-motivated day.

18 TUESDAY   *Moon Age Day 10 Moon Sign Libra*

am ....

pm..

You can now afford to bring enjoyment back into your life and to get in the mood to have fun. The spotlight is on the humorous side of your nature, and it could be one joke after another, all day long. Attending to responsibilities might be the last thing on your mind if you are determined simply to please yourself.

19 WEDNESDAY   *Moon Age Day 11 Moon Sign Libra*

am ....

pm..

Today offers you scope to put the finishing touches to outstanding jobs today, though you might feel that you are not working at your very best. It's a question of ensuring that the deeper recesses of your mind are definitely engaged and that you are using your intuition to the full. Be prepared to examine the motives of others.

20 THURSDAY   *Moon Age Day 12 Moon Sign Scorpio*

am ....

pm..

Pisces is encouraged towards nostalgia now and could spend as much time looking back as it does at the present or the future. If there are valuable lessons to be gained, that's fine. What you don't want is to get stuck into a cycle of activity, simply to replicate matters that you should consider finished and done.

21 FRIDAY
Moon Age Day 13 Moon Sign Scorpio

am ....

pm ....

Communication issues come to the fore today and there are gains to be made if you keep speaking. Even if you don't always know exactly what you are talking about, in a way that doesn't matter. Under current influences you could charm the birds down from the trees, but not if you fail to communicate.

22 SATURDAY
Moon Age Day 14 Moon Sign Sagittarius

am ....

pm ....

Stand by to deal with a few potential irritations today, particularly where work is concerned. Maybe this comes from frustration because you can't get others to see your point of view. Remember that there is always more than one way of looking at any situation. Now is the time to show some of that stoical Piscean patience.

23 SUNDAY
Moon Age Day 15 Moon Sign Sagittarius

am ....

pm ....

The focus now is definitely on your love life and romance generally. Make the most of what could be a very definite 'up' period during which you have what it takes to achieve much of what you have been looking for. Don't spoil this by spending more time than you have to out there in a more practical and go-getting world.

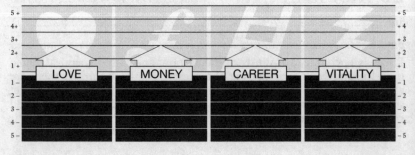

24 MONDAY   *Moon Age Day 16 Moon Sign Capricorn*

am ....

pm ....

In terms of your general ego, today could turn out to be very interesting. This is one of the best days of the month for proving how much your own nature can influence that of other people. Discussions at home are well marked, and have potential to offer much more in a personal sense than outside influences.

25 TUESDAY   *Moon Age Day 17 Moon Sign Capricorn*

am ....

pm ....

If personal relationships seem somewhat less harmonious than you would wish, it's worth asking yourself whether this has anything to do with you. It's important to speak the truth at the moment, even if that means upsetting someone else. All the same, you should be able to find ways to be tactful.

26 WEDNESDAY   *Moon Age Day 18 Moon Sign Aquarius*

am ....

pm ....

Professional matters have much going for them, so turning your attention to out-of-work activities would be no bad thing. Your concern for the underdog is highlighted right now, and this would be an ideal time to show your usual Piscean concern for people who are having a hard time in their life.

27 THURSDAY   ☿   *Moon Age Day 19 Moon Sign Aquarius*

am ....

pm ....

You are now in a position to bring plans to a critical stage, and you won't want to relinquish control to anyone else. This influence can directly interact with another – the desire to share. Out of these conflicting interests you need to forge a way forward that pleases you and everyone else.

28 FRIDAY ☿ *Moon Age Day 20 Moon Sign Pisces*

am ....

pm..

You have a chance to capitalise on a winning streak in both personal and professional matters now. This is far more than just the monthly lunar high, because now you have the planet Mars pulling strongly for you. With energy to spare, lots of ideas available and a positive view of the world, it's onwards and upwards!

29 SATURDAY ☿ *Moon Age Day 21 Moon Sign Pisces*

am ....

pm..

With strong supporting planetary trends and the Moon still within your zodiac sign, now is the moment to act. Any objectives that have been in your sights for some time can be moved forward at a pace, while at the same time you can show yourself and everyone around you how dynamic and decisive you can be.

30 SUNDAY ☿ *Moon Age Day 22 Moon Sign Aries*

am ....

pm..

Professional initiatives are well starred, though you might not be focusing your attention entirely on work on a Sunday. With the summer coming on and the nights light, this would be an ideal time to take up new outdoor interests, perhaps ones that keep you fit as well as generally happy.

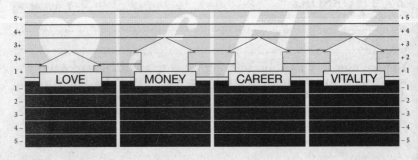

July

2013

Your Month at a Glance

+ = Opportunities are around   ● = Be on the defensive   ○ = Life is pretty ordinary

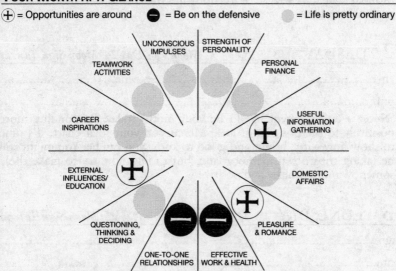

July Highs and Lows

Here I show you how the rhythms of the Moon will affect you this month. Like the tide, your energies and abilities will rise and fall with its pattern. When it is above the centre line, go for it, when it is below, you should be resting.

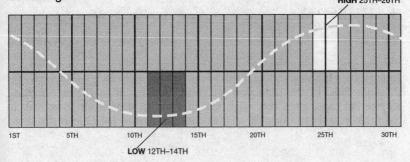

1 MONDAY ☿ *Moon Age Day 23 Moon Sign Aries*

am...

pm...

Trend now indicate disagreements in teamwork issues, either at work or at home. Even if you don't generally expect everyone else to do things the way you think is right, it might be a different matter now. A happy Monday demands a sense of freedom and the chance to follow your own personal rainbow.

2 TUESDAY ☿ *Moon Age Day 24 Moon Sign Taurus*

am...

pm...

'Never a dull moment' could be your motto today. Responding more positively to the position of little Mercury in your solar chart, it's time to show how witty, bright and good to know you can be. You might still be taking trips down memory lane, but should now try to make these somehow more healthy and positive.

3 WEDNESDAY ☿ *Moon Age Day 25 Moon Sign Taurus*

am...

pm...

An ideal day to make some overall improvements at work, and to use your present ability to concentrate on something educational. The better times are really down to you and the way you are presently using your mind. Listening to gossip is all very well, though you need to ask how much of it is really worth the effort.

4 THURSDAY ☿ *Moon Age Day 26 Moon Sign Taurus*

am...

pm...

Energies are highlighted, and this gives you the assistance you need to get through most of the tasks you set yourself today. It might be tempting to bite off more than you can chew in a practical or work sense, but in the main you should be able to find contentment in your life at this time.

5 FRIDAY *Moon Age Day 27 Moon Sign Gemini*

am ....

pm ....

A favourable time to be open to new input, which may be coming from a number of different directions. Adapting yourself to meet new challenges is within your abilities now, and you can also afford to offer a helping hand to less flexible types. Ensure the advice you dish out today is sensible and sound.

6 SATURDAY *Moon Age Day 28 Moon Sign Gemini*

am ....

pm ....

You might have to slow down as far as certain schemes are concerned, particularly if you have been burning the candle at both ends. Thinking matters through carefully should allow you to proceed again, though steadily. The amount of attention you can attract indicates the level of popularity you possess.

7 SUNDAY *Moon Age Day 0 Moon Sign Cancer*

am ....

pm ....

A wonderful ego boost is there for the taking today. The position of Venus gives you the opportunity to elicit some important compliments from those around you. There is nothing half as special as feeling that you are both loved and respected. It is something that Pisces finds difficult to live without.

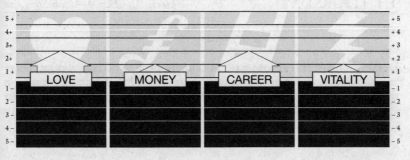

8 MONDAY ☿ *Moon Age Day 1 Moon Sign Cancer*

am ....

pm..

It's possible that professional matters could go askew in a number of different ways, especially if success in this arena depends on other people carrying out specific actions. Concentration is the key, and is the thing that will help you prevent negative trends developing. Most important of all, you need to keep smiling, wherever you are.

9 TUESDAY ☿ *Moon Age Day 2 Moon Sign Cancer*

am ....

pm..

You have scope to make this another progressive day. It's not only a question of getting a great deal done, but also of leaving yourself time to have fun. Mixing business with pleasure ought to be a piece of cake, and even financial matters take on a brighter and more positive perspective under present influences.

10 WEDNESDAY ☿ *Moon Age Day 3 Moon Sign Leo*

am ....

pm..

Romantic offers could available, especially if you are already on the look-out for love. Certainly, your popularity shouldn't be in doubt, but there is nothing especially surprising about that for Pisces. Your natural charm and magnetic personality will help you get noticed, and there is plenty to crow about at the moment.

11 THURSDAY ☿ *Moon Age Day 4 Moon Sign Leo*

am ....

pm..

Domestic matters really do have potential to keep you happy now. There are gains to be made at home, and warmth and kindness to be found in the company of other people. Most of them are simply responding to your naturally affable nature. If you get the chance, do be prepared to sing your own praises today.

12 FRIDAY ☿ *Moon Age Day 5 Moon Sign Virgo*

am..

pm..

The onset of your planetary lull does little more this time than to offer you a brief respite. Take advantage of the situation to spend a little time on your own, something you really need to do now and again. Avoid arguing for any situations that you recognise to be lost causes before you even start.

13 SATURDAY ☿ *Moon Age Day 6 Moon Sign Virgo*

am..

pm..

It pays to keep your life today as free from complications as you can manage. There will be demands to be dealt with, but as long as you are not expecting too much of yourself, you should be able to manage. If you decide to withdraw into your shell at present, you can't expect to be wonderful company at the same time.

14 SUNDAY ☿ *Moon Age Day 7 Moon Sign Virgo*

am..

pm..

As the lunar low starts to retreat, you can be impressive in a personal sense. However, if you are a weekend worker, the signs are less positive. Tensions with work superiors are just one of the possible problems, and all in all, the social side of life suits you best for now. Any slight lack of confidence needn't be allowed to last long.

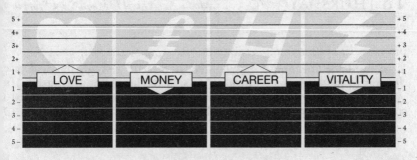

15 MONDAY ☿ *Moon Age Day 8 Moon Sign Libra*

am..

pm..

Today is about doing everything you can to make certain you get noticed. Pisces should be riding on the crest of a wave in terms of personal self-esteem, and you need to make the most of this opportunity. Be prepared to ask for what you want right now because there's a good chance you can get it.

16 TUESDAY ☿ *Moon Age Day 9 Moon Sign Libra*

am..

pm..

Be prepared to step up the pace at work even more than you have been doing of late. Confidence shouldn't be hard to find, and there is much to be said for seeking out some interesting and influential types. This is one of those days when, with just a little care, you might find it hard to put a foot wrong.

17 WEDNESDAY ☿ *Moon Age Day 10 Moon Sign Scorpio*

am..

pm..

Stand by to take advantage of a more co-operative phase generally, including in relation to people who have been somewhat difficult to deal with of late. Taking the line of least resistance in family situations is all very well, though you could well be storing up problems for later. Talk things through honestly right now.

18 THURSDAY ☿ *Moon Age Day 11 Moon Sign Scorpio*

am..

pm..

Your need for affection is highlighted at present, though this will be difficult to fulfil if you are unwilling to spill the beans about yourself. If you want people to understand you, it is important to let down your guard sometimes. Deep, personal relationships are particularly well accented.

19 FRIDAY ☿ *Moon Age Day 12 Moon Sign Sagittarius*

am ....

pm..

This is a period during which you are encouraged to find something new and interesting to occupy your mind and your time. Out there in the big world there are all sorts of offers, and you need to get yourself in just the right frame of mind to say yes to at least some of them. Stand by to put yourself in the public eye soon.

20 SATURDAY ☿ *Moon Age Day 13 Moon Sign Sagittarius*

am ....

pm..

You still need to get ahead with plans, though you are inclined to realise that this might sometimes take a very considered and careful approach. Today Pisces is likely to be looking around, waiting for the best opportunity to act and then doing all that is necessary to win through.

21 SUNDAY *Moon Age Day 14 Moon Sign Capricorn*

am ....

pm..

Don't be surprised if certain personal or practical arrangements are subject to delay now. You need to remain flexible in your attitude and willing to take a different path at very short notice. Casual conversations can allow you to gather some interesting information, or even some really good ideas you will soon be bursting to put into practice.

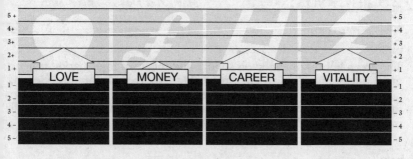

22 MONDAY
Moon Age Day 15 Moon Sign Capricorn

am ....

pm ....

The Sun enters your solar sixth house, a new influence that could have a profound bearing on your working life. All of a sudden you have what it takes to become more organised, and should be planning for new responsibilities that will be available before very long. If you decide to dream today, dream big!

23 TUESDAY
Moon Age Day 16 Moon Sign Aquarius

am ....

pm ....

You would be wise to stick around familiar faces today, particularly if you aren't feeling quite as adventurous as you have been recently. This doesn't mean you have to be a shrinking violet, though you might be tempted to hide behind the personalities of friends. Whatever you do, you can ensure that people want to know you better.

24 WEDNESDAY
Moon Age Day 17 Moon Sign Aquarius

am ....

pm ....

Impressing others shouldn't be too difficult today, and trends assist you to pull the right rabbit out of the hat when it is important to do so. Gaining people's trust is important, though this brings with it the worry that you might let them down. This is most unlikely to happen. Just be yourself and do what feels right.

25 THURSDAY
Moon Age Day 18 Moon Sign Pisces

am ....

pm ....

The green light is on, and you should find the lunar high a good time to make tracks, as well as to gain invaluable assistance on the way. General good luck is there for the taking and offers you the chance to achieve things that have been at the back of your mind for a while. Even if life isn't easy, you can make it interesting.

26 FRIDAY
Moon Age Day 19 Moon Sign Pisces

am ....

pm ....

The lunar high continues, assisting your energy levels no end. You can't expect to achieve everything yourself at this time, even if you are determined to try to do so. A friendly approach towards others will help you to persuade them to follow your opinions, which are generally sensible.

27 SATURDAY
Moon Age Day 20 Moon Sign Aries

am ....

pm ....

When it matters the most you can rely on your instincts today, which are unlikely to let you down. A few financial pressures are possible this weekend, but there are many things you can do that are absolutely free, or which cost very little. Being with friends would be good, but even better times involve your lover.

28 SUNDAY
Moon Age Day 21 Moon Sign Aries

am ....

pm ....

The accent is now less on practical organisation and more on initiative and willpower. You needn't allow much to hold you back at present, once you have made up your mind. There's nothing wrong with using slightly unorthodox ways of getting what you want from the day. You stand every chance of winning through.

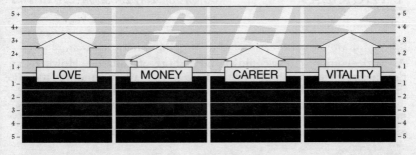

29 MONDAY
Moon Age Day 22 Moon Sign Aries

am ....

pm...

Progress could well be swift now, though you still need to work hard to get things done. It doesn't matter whether there is a professional aspect to today or not, since you can display your capacity for work as much at home as you do anywhere else. Don't forget that you also need to have some fun.

30 TUESDAY
Moon Age Day 23 Moon Sign Taurus

am ....

pm...

Be prepared to get out and travel as much as you can today. Being stuck indoors is not the best use of the day, and you can gain tremendously from seeing new places, as well as from meeting people you haven't come across before. If at all possible, avoid taking on an excessive or stressful workload.

31 WEDNESDAY
Moon Age Day 24 Moon Sign Taurus

am ....

pm...

There are positive social highlights and generally uplifting trends to be experienced out here in the middle of the week. Your powers of communication count for a great deal, and it is possible you are in the mood for debate. Co-operative ventures of any sort are especially well accented at this time.

1 THURSDAY
Moon Age Day 25 Moon Sign Gemini

am ....

pm...

At work, your progress could be little short of fantastic. However, as this means giving much of what you are to the task in hand, fatigue is a distinct possibility by the end of the day. When social hours beckon, it's worth spending some time in the company of people whose presence you find relaxing.

2 FRIDAY
Moon Age Day 26 Moon Sign Gemini

am ....

pm ....

A light and optimistic mood works best now, and assists you in your dealings with new people, but also with family members and friends. With such a sociable period in operation, it might be rather difficult to actually get anything done in a concrete sense. The simple solution would be to split your time.

3 SATURDAY
Moon Age Day 27 Moon Sign Gemini

am ....

pm ....

You can now afford to be quite decisive in your dealings with the outside world. This gives you an opportunity to ensure that nobody is in any doubt as to where you stand. Even if work matters are running smoothly enough, that needn't prevent you from turning your mind towards your social life time and again.

4 SUNDAY
Moon Age Day 28 Moon Sign Cancer

am ....

pm ....

Teamwork situations tend to offer the best potential. This is an ideal time to investigate schemes that others hold in common and make yourself a part of them. Although there may not be quite the level of excitement around that you would wish today, you can at least make steady progress towards your objectives.

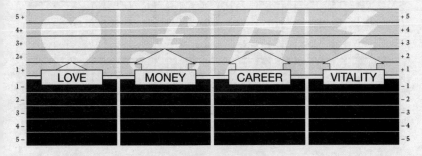

August

2013

Your Month at a Glance

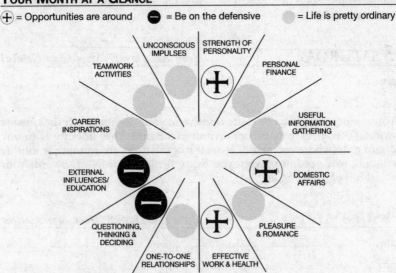

⊕ = Opportunities are around   ⊖ = Be on the defensive   ⬤ = Life is pretty ordinary

STRENGTH OF PERSONALITY

UNCONSCIOUS IMPULSES

TEAMWORK ACTIVITIES

PERSONAL FINANCE

CAREER INSPIRATIONS

USEFUL INFORMATION GATHERING

EXTERNAL INFLUENCES/ EDUCATION

DOMESTIC AFFAIRS

QUESTIONING, THINKING & DECIDING

PLEASURE & ROMANCE

ONE-TO-ONE RELATIONSHIPS

EFFECTIVE WORK & HEALTH

August Highs and Lows

Here I show you how the rhythms of the Moon will affect you this month. Like the tide, your energies and abilities will rise and fall with its pattern. When it is above the centre line, go for it, when it is below, you should be resting.

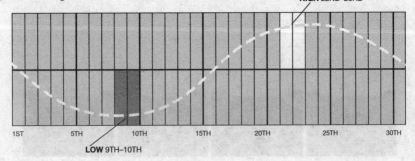

HIGH 22ND–23RD

1ST   5TH   10TH   15TH   20TH   25TH   30TH

LOW 9TH–10TH

5 MONDAY
Moon Age Day 29 Moon Sign Cancer

am ....

pm..

Career matters can now be assisted by the fact that you have options. Of course this might also cloud the issue and make it more likely that you will jump about from foot to foot when making decisions. By all means think about things carefully, but when you have done so, make up your mind and stick to it.

6 TUESDAY
Moon Age Day 0 Moon Sign Leo

am ....

pm..

Make sure you don't alienate others by being too argumentative or assertive today. If certain relationships are rather fragile at the moment, this is the time to consolidate, not to cause waves. Does it feel as though not everyone has your best interests at heart? Bear in mind that you could be misconstruing matters.

7 WEDNESDAY
Moon Age Day 1 Moon Sign Leo

am ....

pm..

This is typically the hottest month of the year, and the fact that summer is well and truly present might provoke a degree of restlessness. Why not get out of the house and do something interesting? Visiting beautiful and tranquil locations can work wonders, especially in the company of some calm relatives or friends!

8 THURSDAY
Moon Age Day 2 Moon Sign Leo

am ....

pm..

If you have managed to bring certain projects near to completion, you may well be looking for something new to do. The right sorts of opportunities are within your reach, though it's possible that your mind is still taken up with the potential for travel. Even short journeys can be of great interest.

9 FRIDAY
Moon Age Day 3 Moon Sign Virgo

am ....

pm..

Your ability to show a distinctly practical face to the world at large may not be at its best today. There is much to be said for seeking help, support and advice from the direction of people you know and trust. During this particular lunar low, you should also seek opportunities to have fun.

10 SATURDAY
Moon Age Day 4 Moon Sign Virgo

am ....

pm..

The potentially quiet patch continues. Rather than fighting against this, you may as well enjoy it. Relax as much as you can and leave some of the more important aspects of life until another time. It's appropriate to put some of your commitments to one side while the lunar low is around.

11 SUNDAY
Moon Age Day 5 Moon Sign Libra

am ....

pm..

This could be a particularly good day when it comes to problem solving. Once you have your Sherlock Holmes hat on, you can turn your mind to something that has been puzzling you for a while. That might even be the behaviour of someone you know well. Perhaps you already hold the answer, but don't realise it.

	LOVE	MONEY	CAREER	VITALITY
5 +				+ 5
4+				+ 4
3+				+ 3
2+				+ 2
1 +				+ 1
1 -				- 1
2 -				- 2
3 -				- 3
4 -				- 4
5 -				- 5

12 MONDAY
Moon Age Day 6 Moon Sign Libra

am ....

pm..

Being in demand can be a very positive experience, though there's a risk that you'll try to spread yourself rather too thinly. Rather than attempting to be all things to all people, it pays to simply be yourself. When you are natural, you can be excellent company. A change in domestic routines would be no bad thing today.

13 TUESDAY
Moon Age Day 7 Moon Sign Scorpio

am ....

pm..

Information could prove invaluable today so it really is worthwhile to keep your eyes and ears open. All sorts of people can now be of use to you, some in ways you could barely guess. Give all new ideas and options good consideration at because help can come from some surprising places.

14 WEDNESDAY
Moon Age Day 8 Moon Sign Scorpio

am ....

pm..

Don't allow important topics to become a hotbed of arguments now. Your best approach is to stay rational and calm, even if there are occasions on which you feel you are being somehow threatened. Avoid animosity, particularly with people who are able to be of great use to you. Tolerance really helps today.

15 THURSDAY
Moon Age Day 9 Moon Sign Scorpio

am ....

pm..

Even if social relationships appear to be working out well at this time, it is in the area of your love life that the real gains can be made. Planetary trends mean that it shouldn't be hard to find the right words to tell someone how much you think about them. Just as important is what you do with the reaction you get in return.

16 FRIDAY
Moon Age Day 10 Moon Sign Sagittarius

am ....

pm...

A new phase comes along, during which you are encouraged to do things in pairs. The Sun is now entering your solar seventh house, where it will stay for the next month. During this time, the more you co-operate, the greater are the rewards on offer. It might not always be easy, but the results make the effort worthwhile.

17 SATURDAY
Moon Age Day 11 Moon Sign Sagittarius

am ....

pm...

Even if you are in great demand socially, you shouldn't feel that you have to become someone else in order to keep attracting the attention. It's important to ensure that you continue to show your true nature, which is what appeals to others in any case. Be prepared to deal with any jealousy or envy that occurs today.

18 SUNDAY
Moon Age Day 12 Moon Sign Capricorn

am ....

pm...

This is not the time to take anything for granted at a practical level, and it's worth checking details carefully. You might get the impression that someone is deliberately throwing obstacles in your path. You need to consider whether this is really the case, or whether your own paranoia has a part to play.

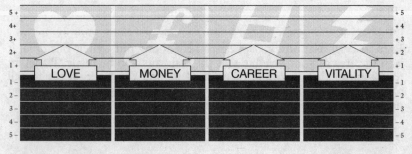

19 MONDAY — *Moon Age Day 13 Moon Sign Capricorn*

am...

pm...

Your best area of influence today is in one-to-one relationships, and these don't necessarily have to be of the romantic sort. Self-employed Pisces people in particular have luck available now. Today offers a chance to stretch yourself and the potential to make financial progress, either now or in the near future.

20 TUESDAY — *Moon Age Day 14 Moon Sign Aquarius*

am...

pm...

With a little financial good fortune available to you around now, you might decide that the time is right to spoil yourself. That's fine, because a little luxury can work wonders. There are good reasons to show your heightened creativity at the moment, perhaps by implementing some major changes at home.

21 WEDNESDAY — *Moon Age Day 15 Moon Sign Aquarius*

am...

pm...

Trends indicate a tendency to retreat from the cut and thrust of everyday life at this time, which is not so strange for the zodiac sign of Pisces. Such behaviour is quite natural when the Moon is residing in your twelfth house as it is today. A quieter approach than usual is your best option for the moment.

22 THURSDAY — *Moon Age Day 16 Moon Sign Pisces*

am...

pm...

You shouldn't have to work very hard to win anyone's support today. The Moon is in your zodiac sign and there are several other planetary positions working in your favour. If you can't get through everything you want to do quick enough to leave time for fun, there's nothing wrong with saving some of it until later.

23 FRIDAY
Moon Age Day 17 Moon Sign Pisces

am ....

pm..

This is certainly a good time to be putting your luck to the test. The lunar high offers a greater chance of success in almost any enterprise, but you will still need grit and determination in order to tackle certain issues. With little or no sense of failure, now is the time to pitch in and succeed.

24 SATURDAY
Moon Age Day 18 Moon Sign Aries

am ....

pm..

You still have what it takes to make the sort of progress that you are definitely looking for at this time. It's a question of showing good and promising judgement, and not being easily put off once you have made up your mind to follow a particular path. Inspiration in your ideas is part of the present package.

25 SUNDAY
Moon Age Day 19 Moon Sign Aries

am ....

pm..

Beware of getting involved in needless debates, which won't help your cause and can only serve to confuse already problematical situations. You can seek help if you need it, though you can also rely on your own efforts and judgement now, so may decide to continue going it alone.

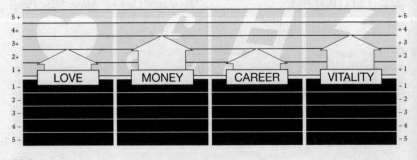

26 MONDAY

Moon Age Day 20 Moon Sign Taurus

am..

pm..

The smooth running of practical affairs today should be your chief concern, as indeed seems to have been the case for a while now. Although circumstances probably force you to work within certain confines, your problem-solving skills are to the fore, and you needn't allow yourself to be distracted by anyone or anything.

27 TUESDAY

Moon Age Day 21 Moon Sign Taurus

am..

pm..

You have scope to find help today, no matter what you decide to do. There are times when you will be responding to necessity, rather than to choice, but the trick is to make these enjoyable too. It's natural to find routines a bore, which is why ringing the changes as much as you can would be no bad thing at the moment.

28 WEDNESDAY

Moon Age Day 22 Moon Sign Gemini

am..

pm..

In personal relationships, it is important not to get too wrapped up in your own ideas, no matter how entrancing they seem to you. You would be wise to use a listening ear and be willing to modify your plans if necessary. A final word of warning for a summer Wednesday – avoid staying in the same place for too long at a time.

29 THURSDAY

Moon Age Day 23 Moon Sign Gemini

am..

pm..

This is potentially the best period for financial gain during August. Acting on impulse is the name of the game, though if you keep your sense of humour fully in place you should be able to laugh your way out of any mistakes you make. The Pisces concern for the underdog is particularly emphasised at the moment.

30 FRIDAY
Moon Age Day 24 Moon Sign Gemini

am ....

pm...

Trends suggest that practical duties could be something of a bind today, so there is much to be said for shrugging them off or delegating them to someone else. However, there are certain responsibilities that cannot be avoided. It's time to grit your teeth and get them done as quickly as possible.

31 SATURDAY
Moon Age Day 25 Moon Sign Cancer

am ....

pm...

Now is as good a time as any to take your life into your own hands. It's a question of knowing what you want and coming up with some good ideas for how you are going to get it. You have scope to turn even apparently unfortunate events to your advantage, and this should give you a racing start as September gets underway.

1 SUNDAY
Moon Age Day 26 Moon Sign Cancer

am ....

pm...

The focus today is predominantly on leisure, and in fact, work could well have been quite low on your agenda for a day or two. Once you've done what is necessary, you can afford to keep the best part of the day for simply enjoying yourself. There's little to be said for taking either yourself or anyone else too seriously at present.

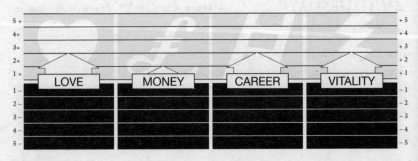

September

2013

YOUR MONTH AT A GLANCE

➕ = Opportunities are around   ⚫ = Be on the defensive   ⬤ = Life is pretty ordinary

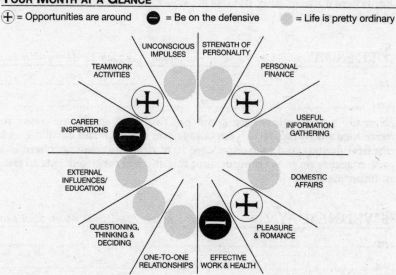

UNCONSCIOUS IMPULSES
STRENGTH OF PERSONALITY
TEAMWORK ACTIVITIES
PERSONAL FINANCE
CAREER INSPIRATIONS
USEFUL INFORMATION GATHERING
EXTERNAL INFLUENCES/ EDUCATION
DOMESTIC AFFAIRS
QUESTIONING, THINKING & DECIDING
ONE-TO-ONE RELATIONSHIPS
EFFECTIVE WORK & HEALTH
PLEASURE & ROMANCE

SEPTEMBER HIGHS AND LOWS

Here I show you how the rhythms of the Moon will affect you this month. Like the tide, your energies and abilities will rise and fall with its pattern. When it is above the centre line, go for it, when it is below, you should be resting.

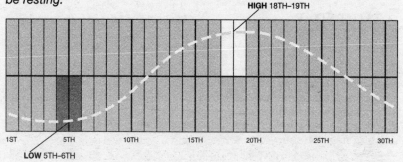

HIGH 18TH–19TH

LOW 5TH–6TH

119

2 MONDAY
Moon Age Day 27 Moon Sign Leo

am ....

pm ....

Speaking your mind is all very well today, though it's worth making sure you know what you are talking about. Rather than getting tied down by too many details, there are gains to be made by taking a broader view of life. Where a whole series of tasks are concerned, do them one at a time and take note of your progress.

3 TUESDAY
Moon Age Day 28 Moon Sign Leo

am ....

pm ....

Be ready to circumnavigate some practical mishaps if you want to move forward today. Trends encourage you to check and double-check practical matters and take extra care with domestic chores. There is a greater accent on travel now, making this an ideal time to decide to take an impromptu trip.

4 WEDNESDAY
Moon Age Day 0 Moon Sign Leo

am ....

pm ....

You should now be able to achieve noticeable improvements in one-to-one relationships, and this can apply even if you had thought everything was fine. Even if rules and regulations don't impress you much at this stage of the working week, that needn't prevent you from telling others what they should be doing.

5 THURSDAY
Moon Age Day 1 Moon Sign Virgo

am ....

pm ....

Important decisions are best left until later. The lunar low encourages you to keep to a minimum your expectations of what you can achieve in life, because your imaginative processes are not at their best right now. You would be wise to settle for a slow and steady sort of day and enjoy as much of it as you can.

6 FRIDAY
Moon Age Day 2 Moon Sign Virgo

am ....

pm ....

Your best approach today is to take life as it comes and don't try to change things too much. Mentally write the word 'Relax' on the inside of your head and look at it as much as you can today. Some of the things you really want are there for the taking, but there is no way you can rush them now.

7 SATURDAY
Moon Age Day 3 Moon Sign Libra

am ....

pm ....

Trends indicate that Pisces can benefit most at present from time spent at home, so this weekend probably isn't the optimum time to be moving around too much. The creative side of your nature is highlighted now, assisting you to tackle jobs in your house or garden. A degree of personal contentment is also possible now.

8 SUNDAY
Moon Age Day 4 Moon Sign Libra

am ....

pm ....

The position of the Moon is likely to stimulate the desire for new experiences today. This is a favourable interlude for spreading your wings, and you can use September well in this regard. A more adventurous spirit generally is now in the air, and the tendency for Pisces to be held back through lack of self-confidence is less marked.

9 MONDAY
Moon Age Day 5 Moon Sign Libra

am ....

pm..

You can now assist career developments by taking the right sort of action. Even if you have to use your famous intuition when deciding how best to deal with specific issues, you still have what it takes to get where you need to be and to impress others on the way. A calm approach works best when speaking in public.

10 TUESDAY
Moon Age Day 6 Moon Sign Scorpio

am ....

pm..

This is another good time to explore the wider social arena, and it must be said that things do go better for you in groups today. It's natural to be somewhat hesitant to commit yourself in a really public arena. It's simply a question of stifling your apprehension and being determined to make a good impression.

11 WEDNESDAY
Moon Age Day 7 Moon Sign Scorpio

am ....

pm..

Once again, activities undertaken with others can work particularly well today. Now is the time to take forward any particular plan or idea that has been on the back burner for some time. Gaining some influential support will help no end in this endeavour. Any sort of overindulgence is best avoided.

12 THURSDAY
Moon Age Day 8 Moon Sign Sagittarius

am ....

pm..

It's possible that Pisces will be in a battling mood at present. Bear in mind that this could well put you on the wrong side of those whose friendship you should be trying to cultivate. It's not that you should allow yourself to be walked on, but there's nothing wrong with giving a little now, in order to get a great deal later.

13 FRIDAY
Moon Age Day 9 Moon Sign Sagittarius

am..

pm..

Socially speaking, there is now a boost available for casual relationships, which is one area of life that might have been slightly overlooked during this year. People you know, but not well, can be of tremendous use to you at the moment. Of course, it isn't a one-way street, so be prepared to give them a leg-up too.

14 SATURDAY
Moon Age Day 10 Moon Sign Capricorn

am..

pm..

If you can find a willing audience at present you shouldn't have too much difficulty in persuading others to follow your lead. This is best accomplished in a fairly quiet way and through example. Although being a leader may not be a natural choice for Pisces, it's a role that you could well be taking on at the moment.

15 SUNDAY
Moon Age Day 11 Moon Sign Capricorn

am..

pm..

There are good reasons to follow the lead and the advice of your partner or a loved one now. Even if this goes against the grain somewhat, you should at least be prepared to listen. If you know in your heart that what they are saying is true, you will lose nothing by compromising, at least in the short term.

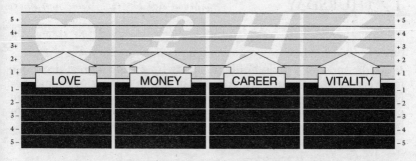

16 MONDAY
Moon Age Day 12 Moon Sign Aquarius

am ....

pm ....

Planning requires time for consideration, though that could be difficult to find today. It is vital to keep moving forward, and you would be wise if you realise this. Allow yourself the right to rest and contemplate for just a while. The lunar high lies around the corner and should make greater confidence available to you.

17 TUESDAY
Moon Age Day 13 Moon Sign Aquarius

am ....

pm ....

Your physical strength might not be exactly up to par today. The Moon in your solar twelfth house encourages you to be more of a spectator than a participant, though this could change dramatically tomorrow. Progress might be sporadic at best, but given the low-key nature of this interlude, will you really care?

18 WEDNESDAY
Moon Age Day 14 Moon Sign Pisces

am ....

pm ....

Be prepared to make this a positive day, with help obtained from not only the people you know, but also those you have barely met. This is not a time for routines, and the lunar high assists you to put in that extra bit of effort that can make all the difference. If you capitalise on the day's potential, progress is a foregone conclusion.

19 THURSDAY
Moon Age Day 15 Moon Sign Pisces

am ....

pm ....

Make the most of a period of high vitality by getting a great deal done in a very short space of time. It might be worth seeking out some new responsibility at this time, or else making yourself available to help out others. Your most important objective today should be that of filling your hours meaningfully.

20 FRIDAY
Moon Age Day 16 Moon Sign Aries

am ....

pm...

It pays to keep some of your ambitions under wraps for the moment, though there is nothing to prevent you from doing some forward planning. By tomorrow, your vitality and sense of urgency will be notable. For now, why not spend time with your partner or family members and let the practical world look after itself?

21 SATURDAY
Moon Age Day 17 Moon Sign Aries

am ....

pm...

Personal attachments offer feelings of warmth and stability, assisting you to make this a generally comfortable Saturday. Your level of confidence should be growing, and you might now find it possible to address certain matters that have been on the back burner of your mind for a while.

22 SUNDAY
Moon Age Day 18 Moon Sign Taurus

am ....

pm...

The best way to keep things in line as far as your personal life is concerned is to stay away from contentious issues. In addition, there are good reasons to dump some past prejudices altogether, which will please some of the people with whom you associate. It ought to be possible to have fun later in the day.

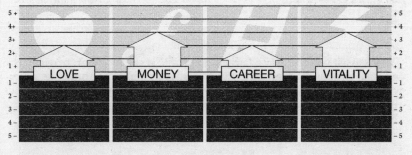

23 MONDAY
Moon Age Day 19   Moon Sign Taurus

am ....

pm ....

There are signs that specific friendships might prove disappointing now, particularly if you find yourself unable to trust certain individuals. Your best approach is simply to shrug your shoulders and move on. If you do feel yourself to be let down in some areas, you need to seek some support in others.

24 TUESDAY
Moon Age Day 20   Moon Sign Taurus

am ....

pm ....

Stand by to make the most of invitations. This is a day when you have everything you need to capitalise on your popularity. Confidence remains to the fore, especially in matters of the heart. The kind streak, which is so much a part of what you are, shouldn't have any trouble in displaying itself today.

25 WEDNESDAY
Moon Age Day 21   Moon Sign Gemini

am ....

pm ....

There could be a slightly hot-tempered aspect to relationships today, at least part of which could be down to your attitude. The fact is that you presently have the planet Mars in a potentially volatile position, and so might have to work hard to keep your temper. In most situations however, you have what it takes to remain calm.

26 THURSDAY
Moon Age Day 22   Moon Sign Gemini

am ....

pm ....

Trends assist you to enjoy a fairly high profile at the moment, particularly in social situations. Your strength lies in your ability to shine like a star when the mood takes you. The flipside is that you might also be fairly sulky if you are prevailed upon to do anything that really goes against the grain.

27 FRIDAY

Moon Age Day 23 Moon Sign Cancer

am...

pm...

Pursing your genuine dreams is the order of the day, especially if you can persuade others to move heaven and earth to support you. In particular, take advantage of favourable influences at work. Bear in mind that if your actions are being closely watched, you need to make sure the impression you create is a positive one.

28 SATURDAY

Moon Age Day 24 Moon Sign Cancer

am...

pm...

Be willing to look within yourself if you encounter problems within your closest relationships. Have you forgotten an anniversary or some other sort of important event? By all means make a few kind gestures, but don't go overboard. You wouldn't want it to seem as though you are crawling.

29 SUNDAY

Moon Age Day 25 Moon Sign Cancer

am...

pm...

Remember there is only so much you can control on your own. The more you are willing to co-operate today, the better the progress you can make. You won't be able to impress everyone, no matter how hard you try. Why not simply try to ignore your reservations and stick with reasonable types?

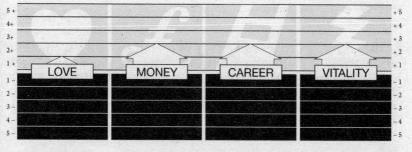

30 MONDAY
Moon Age Day 26 Moon Sign Leo

am ....

pm...

Your competitive nature can now be stimulated by personal encounters. There's no problem here, as long as your opposite number knows how to lose gracefully! You needn't shy away from demands at this time, though it wouldn't be sensible to take on more than is reasonable.

1 TUESDAY
Moon Age Day 27 Moon Sign Leo

am ....

pm...

Your ability to get the best from others is quite noteworthy now. If there is something you particularly want, which can only be supplied by someone else, now is the time to turn on the charm. Be ready to capitalise on the reaction you get, even from people you wouldn't normally try to win round.

2 WEDNESDAY
Moon Age Day 28 Moon Sign Virgo

am ....

pm...

This is a day when you might have to deal with certain limitations, especially within relationships. You need to remember that your judgement may not be up to scratch during the period of the lunar low. The advice is to take what comes, avoid overreacting, and get ready to put things right as soon as you can.

3 THURSDAY
Moon Age Day 29 Moon Sign Virgo

am ....

pm...

As the lunar low continues, limiting your push for progress would be no bad thing. If you don't try to move mountains, you won't be upset when it's impossible to do so. Make the most of a quiet interlude and the chance to do things that please only you. Spending moments on your own may be the best course of action.

4 FRIDAY

Moon Age Day 0 Moon Sign Virgo

am...

pm...

Dealing with personal changes is the order of the day, though these won't necessarily all be of your own choosing. This is a response to the Sun in its present position, though it doesn't have to be a negative scenario. In your free time, there's nothing wrong with seeking a taste of luxury.

5 SATURDAY

Moon Age Day 1 Moon Sign Libra

am...

pm...

A sense of emotional security is possible today, but you won't get away from the fact that general situations are changing rapidly. The creative side of your nature is highlighted at present, so perhaps the time is right for a new look. It's a question of doing something that will persuade others to sit up and take notice.

6 SUNDAY

Moon Age Day 2 Moon Sign Libra

am...

pm...

In practical matters you should be able to find plenty to keep you busy. You have everything you need to create a positive sort of day, though you can't expect everyone to behave in a completely predictable way. Keep a sense of proportion, especially when it comes to looking at matters that might involve financial decisions.

2013

YOUR MONTH AT A GLANCE

(+) = Opportunities are around   ⚫ = Be on the defensive   🔘 = Life is pretty ordinary

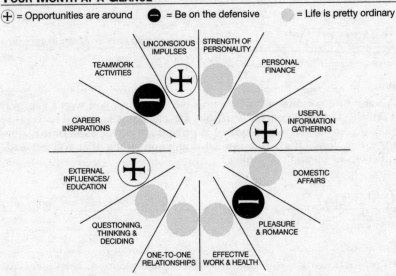

UNCONSCIOUS IMPULSES

STRENGTH OF PERSONALITY

TEAMWORK ACTIVITIES

PERSONAL FINANCE

CAREER INSPIRATIONS

USEFUL INFORMATION GATHERING

EXTERNAL INFLUENCES/ EDUCATION

DOMESTIC AFFAIRS

QUESTIONING, THINKING & DECIDING

PLEASURE & ROMANCE

ONE-TO-ONE RELATIONSHIPS

EFFECTIVE WORK & HEALTH

OCTOBER HIGHS AND LOWS

Here I show you how the rhythms of the Moon will affect you this month. Like the tide, your energies and abilities will rise and fall with its pattern. When it is above the centre line, go for it, when it is below, you should be resting.

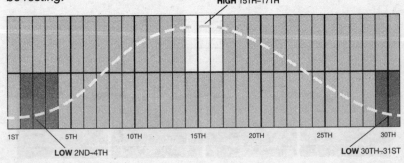

HIGH 15TH–17TH

1ST   5TH   10TH   15TH   20TH   25TH   30TH

LOW 2ND–4TH

LOW 30TH–31ST

7 MONDAY
Moon Age Day 3 Moon Sign Scorpio

am ....

pm ....

A trend that encourages you to turn detective is responsive to little Mercury. This would be an ideal time to discover the ins and outs of every possible situation. What matters the most to you right now is not that things happen, but rather why they happen. Satisfying your curiosity is going to take extra effort, though that shouldn't be a problem.

8 TUESDAY
Moon Age Day 4 Moon Sign Scorpio

am ....

pm ....

Taking a realistic view of what you can achieve should help you today. You will need to find a balance between spending time with family members and friends, and tackling specific tasks that are on your agenda. Allow your confidence to grow again, particularly regarding plans that relate to work.

9 WEDNESDAY
Moon Age Day 5 Moon Sign Sagittarius

am ....

pm ....

Once again, your domestic life could get in the way of the things you want to attend to in the practical world. Even if this appears to be something of a bind, in reality you should be happy to spend time with those you love. Try to avoid crowding your schedule too much, and leave time for your partner in particular.

10 THURSDAY
Moon Age Day 6 Moon Sign Sagittarius

am ....

pm ....

A dramatic period is indicated in terms of your love life. There's a real risk now that matters will be blown up out of all proportion, for whatever reason. Relax! You need to look sensibly at the situation and realise that everything is fine. The one thing you do need to tackle is your present low-key but obvious paranoia.

11 FRIDAY
Moon Age Day 7 Moon Sign Capricorn

am ....

pm..

Do you feel you are in the dark concerning the way other people are behaving? If this does happen to be the case, don't forget that you have a tongue in your head. Rather than struggling to understand matters, your best course of action is to resolve the issue with a word in the right ear.

12 SATURDAY
Moon Age Day 8 Moon Sign Capricorn

am ....

pm..

You can now take advantage of a potentially harmonious period when it comes to your interactions with loved ones. Pisces is a sucker for family, and you are encouraged to show this now. However, it's worth being on your guard against the excessive demands of other people.

13 SUNDAY
Moon Age Day 9 Moon Sign Aquarius

am ....

pm..

Be prepared for a restless streak. Even if the weekend offers plenty in the way of diversion, you might still be seeking more. By all means focus on things that need doing at home, but if this proves difficult, why not opt for travel instead? You may as well get these trips out of the way before winter comes along.

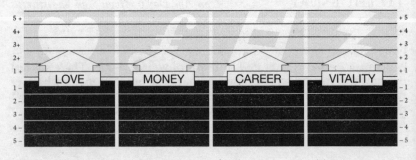

14 MONDAY
Moon Age Day 10 Moon Sign Aquarius

am ....

pm ....

If efficiency is what situations require now, it might be best for you to take a back seat. You don't really have what it takes to be the world's best problem solver while the Moon occupies your solar twelfth house. This is an ideal time for thinking, and period during which stress is best avoided.

15 TUESDAY
Moon Age Day 11 Moon Sign Pisces

am ....

pm ....

A day to make an early start and put in as much time as you can to securing your dreams in the longer term. The lunar high should help and offers a greater degree of confidence. Be prepared to stick your neck out in any situations where you know your attitude to be sensible and your desires modest.

16 WEDNESDAY
Moon Age Day 12 Moon Sign Pisces

am ....

pm ....

If you capitalise on the luck that is available, this can be a very powerful midweek period. Putting in that extra bit of effort at work can help you to get yourself noticed and could make all the difference in the longer term. On the other hand, if you can avoid work altogether today, this would be a great time to have some fun!

17 THURSDAY
Moon Age Day 13 Moon Sign Pisces

am ....

pm ....

Once again, there are gains to be made from finding something new and interesting to do. Freedom of movement is the order of the day, and staying in one place isn't recommended at present. For this reason you might decide to steer clear of domestic situations and instead set out to achieve something quite significant.

18 FRIDAY
Moon Age Day 14 Moon Sign Aries

am ....

pm...

The competitive side of your nature is stimulated and should assist you to maintain your forward thrust. With a sense of purpose and the ability to obtain help when you need it, the desire for progress that has typified your life for a couple of months at least, now seems set to continue.

19 SATURDAY
Moon Age Day 15 Moon Sign Aries

am ....

pm...

The planetary emphasis now is all about broadening your horizons. Even if you can't achieve everything that you want now, you should manage to accumulate most of what you need. Materially speaking, you may have to wait a while before you can begin to push forward more progressively.

20 SUNDAY
Moon Age Day 16 Moon Sign Taurus

am ....

pm...

A little privacy and quiet can work wonders today. However, if you have already committed yourself to a busy Sunday, finding time to be yourself might not be easy. It's not a question of a lack of confidence. Rather, it's simply that for the moment there is much to be gained from enjoying your own company.

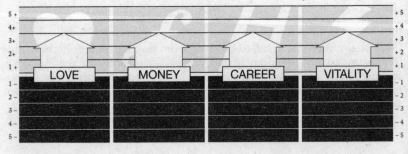

21 MONDAY ☿ *Moon Age Day 17 Moon Sign Taurus*

am...

pm...

A personal matter is likely to put you on the defensive today but do make sure you are not defending yourself before you have even been attacked. The people who matter the most will be on your side at the moment and are unlikely to let you down, even if the going gets a little difficult.

22 TUESDAY ☿ *Moon Age Day 18 Moon Sign Gemini*

am...

pm...

This has potential to be a wonderful time in terms of personal relationships. You can take advantage of quite a few planetary aspects that are now working in your favour, and there is very little to get in the way of romantic bliss. If you are not involved in a personal attachment right now, be prepared to keep your eyes open.

23 WEDNESDAY ☿ *Moon Age Day 19 Moon Sign Gemini*

am...

pm...

If you have to rethink a particular plan of action, you shouldn't view the procedure as being necessarily bad. On the contrary, the more you take your time to consider things right now, the less likelihood there is of making a mistake. Be willing to welcome people you haven't seen for quite some time back into your life.

24 THURSDAY ☿ *Moon Age Day 20 Moon Sign Gemini*

am...

pm...

This may be the best time of this month to have a clear out in your life. Ask yourself whether certain business or social relationships have been holding you back, and whether specific people simply don't have your best interests at heart. It's not about being hard-hearted, but about looking objectively at situations.

25 FRIDAY ☿ *Moon Age Day 21 Moon Sign Cancer*

am ....

pm ....

Outdoor pursuits are especially well highlighted now, and the more sporting and competitive side of your nature also comes to the fore. If you are able to summon up plenty of courage, this would be an ideal period in which to tackle any issues that have had you quaking in your boots at some stage in the past.

26 SATURDAY ☿ *Moon Age Day 22 Moon Sign Cancer*

am ....

pm ....

This would be a favourable time to bring something to a successful conclusion, a possible scenario that has been around for most of the week but which looks even more pertinent now. Be on the look-out for ways to improve your life and also your finances. A change of scene would probably be welcome.

27 SUNDAY ☿ *Moon Age Day 23 Moon Sign Leo*

am ....

pm ....

It can benefit you greatly to keep in touch with people who are in the know. Your generally affable ways should help you to maintain your popularity, and you can turn this fact to your advantage by calling in some assistance. Material progress is now possible as you move towards the culmination of plans you hatched some time ago.

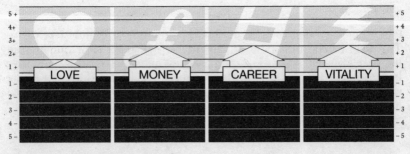

28 MONDAY ☿ *Moon Age Day 24 Moon Sign Leo*

am ....

pm...

Some emotional issues can seem to be more trouble than they are worth. However, you should still be willing to give an airing to any crucial matters between yourself and those you love. Of course, a tactful approach is the order of the day, but you shouldn't leave things alone if they might deteriorate further.

29 TUESDAY ☿ *Moon Age Day 25 Moon Sign Leo*

am ....

pm...

You could find that certain decisions have an element of trial and error about them at the moment. Even if this is a fact you can't get away from, you can at least ensure that it works in your best interests as much as possible. Although the argumentative side of your nature isn't emphasised at present, you need to make sure you are heard.

30 WEDNESDAY ☿ *Moon Age Day 26 Moon Sign Virgo*

am ....

pm...

The lunar low encourages a cautious approach, and one in which you should steer clear of any type of risk or gamble. This means that any major decisions are best left for a few days. If this isn't possible, be prepared to check the details very carefully and seek advice from someone you trust.

31 THURSDAY ☿ *Moon Age Day 27 Moon Sign Virgo*

am ....

pm...

The restrictions continue today, and there isn't much point in ignoring the fact. There are moments when it is sensible to push against pressure, but this probably isn't one of them. Simply watch and wait for a day or two, being prepared to move only when you are really convinced that the time is right.

1 FRIDAY ☿ *Moon Age Day 28 Moon Sign Libra*

am ....

pm...

Close, emotional involvement can now offer more satisfaction than ever. You don't necessarily have to settle for a quiet Friday, though you might decide to use it to show loved ones how important they are to you. Your sense of balance is well accented, assisting you to know instinctively how and when to take action.

2 SATURDAY ☿ *Moon Age Day 0 Moon Sign Libra*

am ....

pm...

You have what it takes to make social affairs a breeze at the moment. The spotlight is on your ability to get on well with the crowd, and any shyness that typifies Pisces can be put to one side for the moment. Don't be in too much of a rush to complete specific jobs. It might be best to wait a while to make sure it is done properly.

3 SUNDAY ☿ *Moon Age Day 1 Moon Sign Scorpio*

am ....

pm...

One-to-one relationships can be a source of warmth and security for you right now, whereas you may be facing difficulties in more distant attachments. Even if confidence isn't easy to find, you should be able to do what is necessary to get ahead, without showing others that you are quaking inside!

5 +						+ 5
4+						+ 4
3+						+ 3
2+						+ 2
1 +	LOVE	MONEY	CAREER	VITALITY		+ 1
1 –						– 1
2 –						– 2
3 –						– 3
4 –						– 4
5 –						– 5

November

2013

YOUR MONTH AT A GLANCE

⊕ = Opportunities are around ⊖ = Be on the defensive ● = Life is pretty ordinary

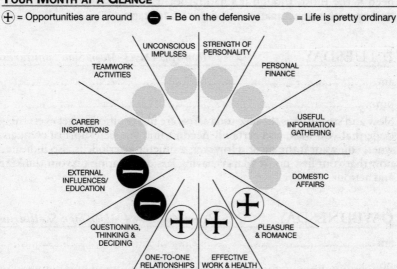

UNCONSCIOUS IMPULSES

STRENGTH OF PERSONALITY

TEAMWORK ACTIVITIES

PERSONAL FINANCE

CAREER INSPIRATIONS

USEFUL INFORMATION GATHERING

EXTERNAL INFLUENCES/ EDUCATION

DOMESTIC AFFAIRS

QUESTIONING, THINKING & DECIDING

PLEASURE & ROMANCE

ONE-TO-ONE RELATIONSHIPS

EFFECTIVE WORK & HEALTH

NOVEMBER HIGHS AND LOWS

Here I show you how the rhythms of the Moon will affect you this month. Like the tide, your energies and abilities will rise and fall with its pattern. When it is above the centre line, go for it, when it is below, you should be resting.

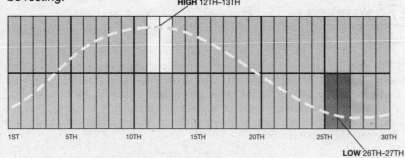

HIGH 12TH–13TH

1ST   5TH   10TH   15TH   20TH   25TH   30TH

LOW 26TH–27TH

4 MONDAY ☿ *Moon Age Day 2 Moon Sign Scorpio*

am ....

pm..

Most of what happens in terms of general progress should be successful if you use your coercive charm and your ability to get to the heart of any matter, especially in a personal sense. Confidence is available when you need it the most, though it's natural for it to flag somewhat if you are dealing with subject matter you don't understand.

5 TUESDAY ☿ *Moon Age Day 3 Moon Sign Sagittarius*

am ....

pm..

Slow and steady wins the race today. You are in a position to get everything done that you wish, and certainly needn't find yourself short of company when you want it the most. However, a quieter interlude is also indicated now that your first-house Mars is having less of a bearing on your thinking and actions.

6 WEDNESDAY ☿ *Moon Age Day 4 Moon Sign Sagittarius*

am ....

pm..

It looks as though your ego is to the fore at the present time, and this should assist you to convince others that your opinions and instructions are sound. Not having to argue the point or to explain yourself time and again can be quite important. It might even allow you to complete tasks in record time.

7 THURSDAY ☿ *Moon Age Day 5 Moon Sign Capricorn*

am ....

pm..

Social life and pleasure pursuits can allow you to make life both busy and interesting today. All the same, do ensure that you are not burning the candle at both ends, which is always a possibility as far as you are concerned. There are signs that being the main attraction could suit you down to the ground now.

YOUR DAILY GUIDE TO NOVEMBER 2013

8 FRIDAY ☿ *Moon Age Day 6 Moon Sign Capricorn*

am...

pm...

Broadening your personal horizons is the name of the game right now.
The spotlight is on intellectual and cultural interests, and these give you
the chance to pursue a different sort of Friday from the one you might
have expected. You are now nearing the end of an important phase in
your life and need to plan ahead.

9 SATURDAY ☿ *Moon Age Day 7 Moon Sign Aquarius*

am...

pm...

Good news could so easily be available today, possibly associated with
a career development. It's natural to feel excited about such positive
scenarios, though it really does pay to wait and see. The true qualities of
Pisces now count for a great deal, so you can display patience as a matter
of routine.

10 SUNDAY ☿ *Moon Age Day 8 Moon Sign Aquarius*

am...

pm...

Furthering personal objectives could be on your agenda this Sunday. If
you feel you would benefit from a rest, today could offer you the ideal
opportunity, thought this might not last for long. Be ready to respond
positively if people are coming to you for help and assistance.

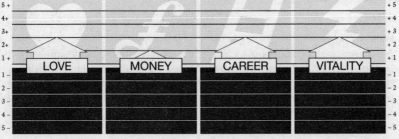

11 MONDAY ☿ *Moon Age Day 9 Moon Sign Aquarius*

am ....

pm ....

This is a favourable time for getting down to business. Mars remains in a strong position for you and offers both incentive and know-how. By now you should have made it clear that you are no pushover, and that others need to keep their wits about them when dealing with you. All in all, this helps you to gain respect.

12 TUESDAY *Moon Age Day 10 Moon Sign Pisces*

am ....

pm ....

With the lunar high comes renewed enthusiasm for projects that could have been taking a back seat across the last couple of weeks. Now you have the chance to turn some ideas into hard fact. When you need assistance to do so, your best approach is to turn to those people who have been your best supporters all along.

13 WEDNESDAY *Moon Age Day 11 Moon Sign Pisces*

am ....

pm ....

At least today you needn't allow much to stand in your way in a general sense. It appears that you have everything to play for, coupled with the ability to persuade others to lend a hand when it matters the most. The lunar high assists you to inspire confidence, which proves to be very important when there is so much going on.

14 THURSDAY *Moon Age Day 12 Moon Sign Aries*

am ....

pm ....

New personal relationships can be given a welcome and timely boost because of the present position of Venus in your solar chart. Although the lunar high is now out of the way, spending too much time on your own is still not to be recommended. You can afford to seek out bright lights and interesting people.

15 FRIDAY

Moon Age Day 13 Moon Sign Aries

am ....

pm..

In a professional sense you would be wise to watch your back in case there are people around who don't have your best interests at heart. This fact could sap your confidence, though probably not for long. Today works best if you pace yourself and avoid trying to get everything done at the same time.

16 SATURDAY

Moon Age Day 14 Moon Sign Taurus

am ....

pm..

A breath of fresh air can work wonders now. Putting in plenty of hard work is all very well, but you need to consider whether you've been getting a sufficient amount of relaxation for a Pisces person. There is much to be said now for getting away from responsibilities and finding some time to please yourself.

17 SUNDAY

Moon Age Day 15 Moon Sign Taurus

am ....

pm..

Your thirst for information and new ideas knows no bounds right now. Creative potential remains emphasised, and romance could well play a part in your Sunday. It's time to let your personality shine, and to enjoy the positive feedback you can attract, including from some quite surprising directions.

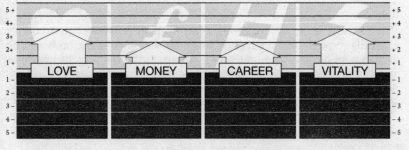

18 MONDAY
Moon Age Day 16 Moon Sign Taurus

am ....

pm..

If you wake feeling exhausted today, you must remember the old adage that a change is as good as a rest. Try to do different things and, where possible, get a true holiday from everyday routines. You have what it takes to convince certain people to assist you, and may relish the time for contemplation this offers.

19 TUESDAY
Moon Age Day 17 Moon Sign Gemini

am ....

pm..

There are gains to be made in the professional world, not least in the light of new information that is available to you at any time now. It pays to start planning for any special occasions that are about to happen. Beware of pushing too hard against insurmountable odds.

20 WEDNESDAY
Moon Age Day 18 Moon Sign Gemini

am ....

pm..

Getting your own way in personal relationships ought to be fairly easy at present. All you have to do is to turn on the charm and then wait to see the results. A day to keep life running fairly smoothly and capitalise on the interesting possibilities that are within your grasp in a social sense.

21 THURSDAY
Moon Age Day 19 Moon Sign Cancer

am ....

pm..

Variety is the spice of life, though you need to remember that you are primarily responsible for keeping things on the move at the moment. An exchange of ideas can be quite illuminating during the present interlude, and could persuade you to modify your own thinking regarding a fairly important issue.

22 FRIDAY

Moon Age Day 20 Moon Sign Cancer

am ....

pm...

Be ready to deal with any problems that arise today, particularly in relation to your over-emotional tendencies. You would be well advised to use your practical common sense, rather than to allow your naturally kind ways to influence your judgement. Paying attention is the best way to avoid being taken for a ride.

23 SATURDAY

Moon Age Day 21 Moon Sign Leo

am ....

pm...

You have scope to make contact with some new and interesting people at the moment. If you haven't already taken this fact into account, maybe you should do so today. Whether you meet these people at work, or within your home life, you can get a great deal out of new encounters. These could furnish you with schemes and plans for next year.

24 SUNDAY

Moon Age Day 22 Moon Sign Leo

am ....

pm...

You have scope to make today very interesting, though you may need to deal with a few small setbacks. It is possible that in the middle of enjoying yourself, there might actually be a requirement for you to do some work! If this really isn't the way you are feeling, simply find ways and means of avoiding it.

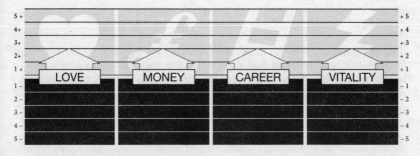

25 MONDAY
Moon Age Day 23 Moon Sign Leo

am ....

pm...

Out there in the social mainstream is the place to be today, even if that is not exactly what you had planned. At every level you can afford to allow work to take something of a back seat in favour of having fun. Confidence shouldn't be lacking, especially if you make a point of mixing with people who make you feel good.

26 TUESDAY
Moon Age Day 24 Moon Sign Virgo

am ....

pm...

This probably isn't the most progressive day of the month. The lunar low can promote a rather sluggish interlude, and could also persuade you to postpone projects you have been planning for a while. Make the day your own by doing exactly what takes your fancy. If that means curling up with a book, then so be it.

27 WEDNESDAY
Moon Age Day 25 Moon Sign Virgo

am ....

pm...

You can't expect absolutely everything to go ahead strictly as you might have wished. The lunar low is inclined to stop you in your tracks, often at a stage in affairs that seems quite important. There should be moments today during which you can think, and that is a positive thing.

28 THURSDAY
Moon Age Day 26 Moon Sign Libra

am ....

pm...

Rather than spending too much time today thinking about what you want for yourself, you need to find ways of addressing the needs and wants of loved ones. This is the truly unselfish quality of Pisces, which is never really very far from the surface. Your intuition works well, particularly if you are dealing with strangers.

29 FRIDAY

Moon Age Day 27 Moon Sign Libra

am ....

pm..

Your go-ahead frame of mind is still to the fore, though you might be showing this in a slightly different way now. Trends now highlight your ability to cheer up even the grumpiest of people. Your sense of humour can be especially infectious, and you have a natural wisdom that should be there for all to see.

30 SATURDAY

Moon Age Day 28 Moon Sign Libra

am ....

pm..

You need to broaden your horizons as much as possible and avoid being in any way restricted in your thinking. Pisces has potential to be very creative in terms of ideas around now, a factor that can stand you in good stead, both at home and work. It pays to keep abreast of current affairs.

1 SUNDAY

Moon Age Day 29 Moon Sign Scorpio

am ....

pm..

Opportunities for overall gain are available. Breaking down barriers and gaining plenty of personal freedom is all very well, though you should make sure that you don't neglect the financial aspects of life. Avoid listening to either rumours or gossip, since there's no guarantee that either of these are totally accurate.

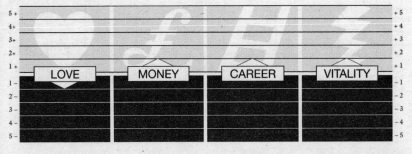

December

2013

YOUR MONTH AT A GLANCE

(+) = Opportunities are around   (−) = Be on the defensive   ● = Life is pretty ordinary

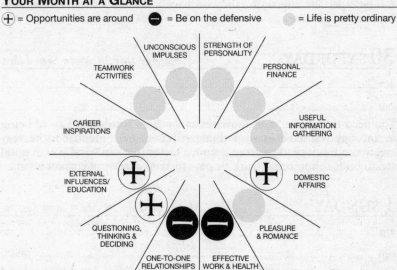

DECEMBER HIGHS AND LOWS

Here I show you how the rhythms of the Moon will affect you this month. Like the tide, your energies and abilities will rise and fall with its pattern. When it is above the centre line, go for it, when it is below, you should be resting.

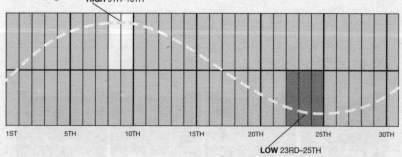

HIGH 9TH–10TH

LOW 23RD–25TH

2 MONDAY
Moon Age Day 0 Moon Sign Scorpio

am ....

pm ....

This can be a favourable day from a professional point of view, with scope to make allies at every stage. Your continued reliance on a specific individual could now lead to one or two problems, especially if the person concerned fails to live up to your expectations. It's time to embark on new projects with as much confidence as you can muster.

3 TUESDAY
Moon Age Day 1 Moon Sign Sagittarius

am ....

pm ....

Contacts with superiors at work could help you to reach a better understanding, and might even prove advantageous to you personally in the fullness of time. Make the most of the chance to complete any tasks that seem to have been dragging on. After all, this should give you more time to do other things.

4 WEDNESDAY
Moon Age Day 2 Moon Sign Sagittarius

am ....

pm ....

You can't expect life to organise itself, particularly at work. You may have to pitch in early in the day, particularly if there are specific issues to sort out. Now is the time to show the typical Piscean good humour and understanding. It should help you to attend to things today and maintain a happy frame of mind.

5 THURSDAY
Moon Age Day 3 Moon Sign Capricorn

am ....

pm ....

A boost to career-based matters is there for the taking now. The Sun in your solar tenth house assists you to look ahead of yourself with a determination to make the most of any opportunity that comes your way. Most important of all, you can afford to be extremely decisive.

149

6 FRIDAY
Moon Age Day 4 Moon Sign Capricorn

am ....

pm ....

Once again you are encouraged to look ahead – far ahead in some cases. This long-term view is quite typical of your sign as a rule though it may not have figured strongly of late. Another sphere of interest right now will be the plans you are laying down for the festive season, particularly with regard to younger people.

7 SATURDAY
Moon Age Day 5 Moon Sign Aquarius

am ....

pm ....

Friendship and group-related matters have a great deal to offer this weekend. There are gains to be made by getting your thinking cap for the Christmas period, so time spent arranging things today will not be wasted. Most Pisceans should be determined to make the upcoming holidays as perfect as possible.

8 SUNDAY
Moon Age Day 6 Moon Sign Aquarius

am ....

pm ....

If you can keep the wheels of progress turning smoothly enough, you should be in a position to make this an interesting and eventful sort of Saturday. A shopping spree would be no bad thing if the pre-Christmas crowds don't worry you. Maybe you can become a professional people watcher!

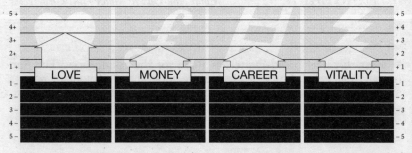

9 MONDAY

Moon Age Day 7 Moon Sign Pisces

am ....

pm...

The lunar high brings potential for a heightened sense of enthusiasm and opportunity to have fun. It's time to go for what you want, especially at work, and refuse to allow yourself to be slowed down by negativity on the part of other people. It is very important for you to know that you are forging your own path now.

10 TUESDAY

Moon Age Day 8 Moon Sign Pisces

am ....

pm...

This is the second day in a row with the Moon in your own zodiac sign. At least at the beginning of the day that offers you extra incentive, probably enough to carry you successfully on until the evening. Rather than getting bogged down with details today, remember that it is the overall picture that matters.

11 WEDNESDAY

Moon Age Day 9 Moon Sign Aries

am ....

pm...

The accent today is on your ability to take charge once more. If you are bringing long-term tasks to their ultimate conclusion, you need to be looking for new possibilities. Be ready to respond if you discover that some friends have a specific need of you at the moment. Listen to what they have to say and act accordingly.

12 THURSDAY

Moon Age Day 10 Moon Sign Aries

am ....

pm...

Look out for new opportunities to broaden your horizons in some way today, probably on a social footing. It shouldn't be too difficult to mix business with pleasure, and you have everything you need to make the best of all impressions on practically everyone you meet during the coming hours.

13 FRIDAY
Moon Age Day 11 Moon Sign Taurus

am ....

pm ....

It's important to identify where there is scope for advancement, even if you can't actually make progress today. Now is the time to get your thinking cap on and plan ahead as carefully as you can. You needn't settle for second-best in terms of new responsibilities. Do everything to the best of your ability.

14 SATURDAY
Moon Age Day 12 Moon Sign Taurus

am ....

pm ....

Trends now suggest that you can derive the greatest joys in life from co-operation with others. Group activities are the name of the game, which is probably not surprising so near to Christmas. Be willing to find ways and means to enjoy yourself, and look for opportunities to bring joy to as many people as possible.

15 SUNDAY
Moon Age Day 13 Moon Sign Taurus

am ....

pm ....

The things that are the most enjoyable now are to be found out there in the wider world. With plenty to play for and more than a modicum of good luck on your side, you can still afford to back your hunches. Contact with people you haven't seen for some time is favoured, and there is much to be gained from any such interaction.

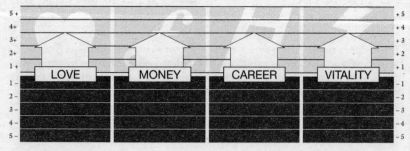

16 MONDAY
Moon Age Day 14 Moon Sign Gemini

am ....

pm...

The spotlight is on your need for independence as this new working week gets underway. Even if being told what to do doesn't appeal, if superiors are involved you probably won't have too much choice. It's time to look ahead in terms of travel plans, even well into next year if possible.

17 TUESDAY
Moon Age Day 15 Moon Sign Gemini

am ....

pm...

A matter associated with love may give you pause for thought. However, since there is such an emphasis on social matters now, you might not have too much time to think about it. Confidence shouldn't be lacking, and there is much to be said for putting some genuine effort into medium- and long-term planning.

18 WEDNESDAY
Moon Age Day 16 Moon Sign Cancer

am ....

pm...

By all means look at the ideas of others now, but if these don't appeal, be ready to think in terms of your own schemes. Whether or not you can bring important people round to your way of thinking remains to be seen. There are some quite significant changes on offer for some Pisces people.

19 THURSDAY
Moon Age Day 17 Moon Sign Cancer

am ....

pm...

Today works best if you can focus on the more practical aspects of life. There are signs that you will want to do your own thing today and won't take kindly to being bossed around. The end of a particular phase in your life is approaching, and although this could provoke some nostalgia, the gains should outweigh the losses.

20 FRIDAY
Moon Age Day 18   Moon Sign Cancer

am ....

pm ....

Even if you are determined to stay on the move today, beware of allowing distractions to get in the way of real, financial progress. Dragging yourself back to practicalities might not seem too inspiring, but could prove to be quite important all the same. It is also a good time to get your Christmas head on.

21 SATURDAY
Moon Age Day 19   Moon Sign Leo

am ....

pm ....

So close to Christmas, the overriding desire at the moment is to find a degree of personal freedom, a concern that has probably been on your mind for a few weeks now. It's time for Pisces to break the old moulds and look for a slightly different identity. You can use events in the outside world to help you in this process.

22 SUNDAY
Moon Age Day 20   Moon Sign Leo

am ....

pm ....

You have what it takes to keep up a fast pace of events in the professional or practical world today. There is vital information there for the taking and you shouldn't be slow to pick up on what others are trying to tell you. By all means give yourself a pat on the back for a recent personal success, but don't let it go to your head!

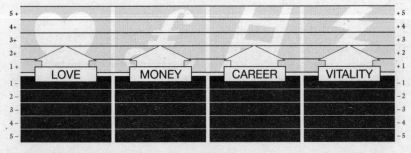

23 MONDAY
Moon Age Day 21 Moon Sign Virgo

am...

pm...

Faces old and new could be encountered now, immediately ahead of the Christmas period. The lunar low makes a trip down memory lane more likely, which is fine, because that's what Christmas is all about. With only two days to go, this would be a good time to review the arrangements you have made.

24 TUESDAY
Moon Age Day 22 Moon Sign Virgo

am...

pm...

The strengthening lunar low becomes more apparent today, as quieter trends generally prove to be the norm. Maintaining a happy frame of mind is a question of keeping yourself occupied through this interlude. What might be more difficult now is to overturn obstacles. Why not get some rest, perhaps in a family setting?

25 WEDNESDAY
Moon Age Day 23 Moon Sign Virgo

am...

pm...

Right now you should sit back and enjoy what Christmas Day has to offer. Actually, there may not be a great deal else you can do. The lunar low does little for your energy levels, and could dissuade you from pushing forward with the verve or enthusiasm you've become accustomed to having. Never mind – enjoy the break!

26 THURSDAY
Moon Age Day 24 Moon Sign Libra

am...

pm...

Even if your interactions with others don't turn out to be universally as enjoyable as you may have wished, Boxing Day can have its benefits. For one thing it's a chance to find out for definite how those around you are feeling. Be prepared to gather some positive feedback, and to feel extremely special at this time.

27 FRIDAY
Moon Age Day 25 Moon Sign Libra

am ....

pm..

Even if you choose to stay indoors and soak up the Christmas spirit, you still have potential to make this a particularly positive and enjoyable day. Travel is probably best postponed for a day or two. For the moment, your overriding need is to feel warm, secure and surrounded by love.

28 SATURDAY
Moon Age Day 26 Moon Sign Scorpio

am ....

pm..

This would be an ideal time to enjoy the company of others for its own sake. Today works best if you are willing to approach it with no agenda, and are happy to simply 'be'. This is a concept that is more understandable to Pisces than any other of the twelve zodiac signs.

29 SUNDAY
Moon Age Day 27 Moon Sign Scorpio

am ....

pm..

As you grow more and more confident, so you should feel less intimidated if you find yourself in the limelight. Your actions today can attract some favourable reactions, and you need to make the most of this situation. Today is also good for all aspects of romance and one-to-one encounters.

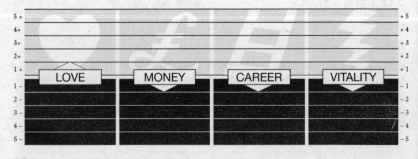

30 MONDAY   *Moon Age Day 28 Moon Sign Sagittarius*

am..

pm..

Ask yourself whether there is any sense in arguing the toss about specific matters if that means upsetting those around you. Medium- and longer-term issues are best put on hold, so that you can give most of your attention to enjoying what the holidays have to offer. Younger people could well figure in your thinking today.

31 TUESDAY   *Moon Age Day 29 Moon Sign Sagittarius*

am..

pm..

'The more, the merrier' might be the best adage for today. All encounters are well marked, and love especially could play a significant part in your thinking and actions. Look out for some good news coming from friends. This can enhance your optimism when it comes to looking at the new year that lies ahead of you.

RISING SIGNS FOR PISCES

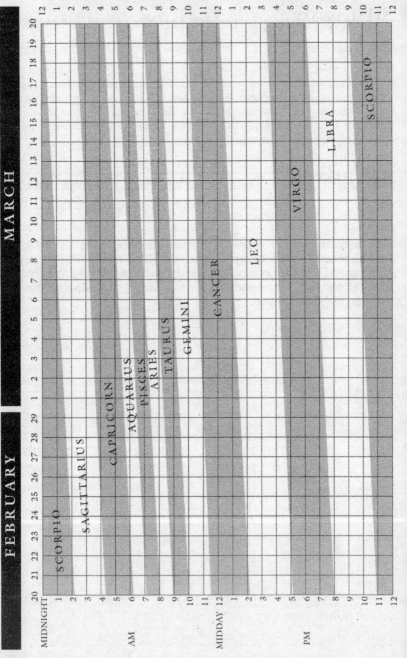

THE ZODIAC, PLANETS AND CORRESPONDENCES

The Earth revolves around the Sun once every calendar year, so when viewed from Earth the Sun appears in a different part of the sky as the year progresses. In astrology, these parts of the sky are divided into the signs of the zodiac and this means that the signs are organised in a circle. The circle begins with Aries and ends with Pisces.

Taking the zodiac sign as a starting point, astrologers then work with all the positions of planets, stars and many other factors to calculate horoscopes and birth charts and tell us what the stars have in store for us.

The table below shows the planets and Elements for each of the signs of the zodiac. Each sign belongs to one of the four Elements: Fire, Air, Earth or Water. Fire signs are creative and enthusiastic; Air signs are mentally active and thoughtful; Earth signs are constructive and practical; Water signs are emotional and have strong feelings.

It also shows the metals and gemstones associated with, or corresponding with, each sign. The correspondence is made when a metal or stone possesses properties that are held in common with a particular sign of the zodiac.

Finally, the table shows the opposite of each star sign – this is the opposite sign in the astrological circle.

Placed	Sign	Symbol	Element	Planet	Metal	Stone	Opposite
1	Aries	Ram	Fire	Mars	Iron	Bloodstone	Libra
2	Taurus	Bull	Earth	Venus	Copper	Sapphire	Scorpio
3	Gemini	Twins	Air	Mercury	Mercury	Tiger's Eye	Sagittarius
4	Cancer	Crab	Water	Moon	Silver	Pearl	Capricorn
5	Leo	Lion	Fire	Sun	Gold	Ruby	Aquarius
6	Virgo	Maiden	Earth	Mercury	Mercury	Sardonyx	Pisces
7	Libra	Scales	Air	Venus	Copper	Sapphire	Aries
8	Scorpio	Scorpion	Water	Pluto	Plutonium	Jasper	Taurus
9	Sagittarius	Archer	Fire	Jupiter	Tin	Topaz	Gemini
10	Capricorn	Goat	Earth	Saturn	Lead	Black Onyx	Cancer
11	Aquarius	Waterbearer	Air	Uranus	Uranium	Amethyst	Leo
12	Pisces	Fishes	Water	Neptune	Tin	Moonstone	Virgo

TALISMAN OF THE SEVEN ANGELS

Created by the Circle of Raphael

Invite Seven Angels into Your Life Today with the Aid of this Lucky Angelic Pendant Talisman of the Seven Angels. ONLY £21.50 plus p&p.

Individually crafted in solid sterling silver. Order today and receive a FREE chain.

Angels are highly positive Cosmic beings and they will not usually step into a person's life without first being invited to do so. This Angelic lucky pendant, inscribed in the divine Angelic language of the Cosmos and imbued with the sacred holy words of creation, was revealed to the Mystic of the *Circle of Raphael* by the Angels themselves. The sacred holy words and Angel names embedded in the pendant are what make it so special. Ownership of this lucky Angelic prayer pendant invites each one of the Seven Angels to befriend its owner and bless and protect them. Over the years we have received numerous testimonials in the form of letters and emails from extremely pleased and astounded owners of this lucky Angelic pendant. To view our genuine testimonials please visit our website.

To fulfil their own spiritual destiny, Angels need to give of themselves and assist anyone who requests their help. However, they first need you to personally invite them into your life so they can fulfil their divine purpose. The most direct and successful way of inviting Angels into your life is to simply wear or carry this holy Angelic pendant calling on the Seven Angels using their personal holy name asking each of them to befriend, watch over and protect the wearer every day of their life. The following is a list of the Angelic gifts associated with each of the Seven Angels named on the pendant plus the true holy name of each Angel written in Angelic script and translated into English:

(ש) ZAPHAEL – Inner peace and happiness.
(ג) GABRIEL – Divine protection and safety in travel.
(ז) HANIEL – Luck in love and relationships.
(ת) RAPHAEL – Financial security and good health.
(ח) CHAMAEL – Protection from acts of violence.
(ב) ZADKIEL – Good fortune in games of chance.
(ר) MICHAEL – Angelic help in career and work.

Wear or carry this lucky Angelic prayer in the form of a pendant and personally invite the Seven Angels to befriend you and enter your life. This one lucky Angelic pendant also invites all Seven Angels to act as your personal Angelic ally in times of need.

We charge only one £4.50 postage & packing fee no matter how many pendants you order at the same time for delivery to the same address. So why not order an extra one for a friend or loved one and save on the postage? **To order by post:** Send your name and address plus your cheque, postal order or debit/credit card details **made payable to: C.O. Raphael.**

Send to: C.O. RAPHAEL (OMH) P.O. BOX 73, ST AUSTELL, PL26 8SH, UK

UK Postage & Packing: Please add £4.50 to your order. **Airmail P&P Outside UK:** Add £8.00 to your order. Do **NOT** send cash under any circumstances.

FAST ORDER ONLINE AT:

www.circleraphael.co.uk

Order With Confidence – This miraculous Seven Angel pendant is covered by our unique 60-day guarantee of full satisfaction or your money back – less the postage & packing fee paid.